# THANK YOU FOR PURCHASING MY THIRD ARTBOOK!

Please enjoy the art I've featured in this book! Although my art goals have since shifted to new projects, I am still glad to have had the opportunity to continue to create. A lot has changed, but I am still chasing dreams, and I intend to keep drawing!

*Princess Reimina Keishana*

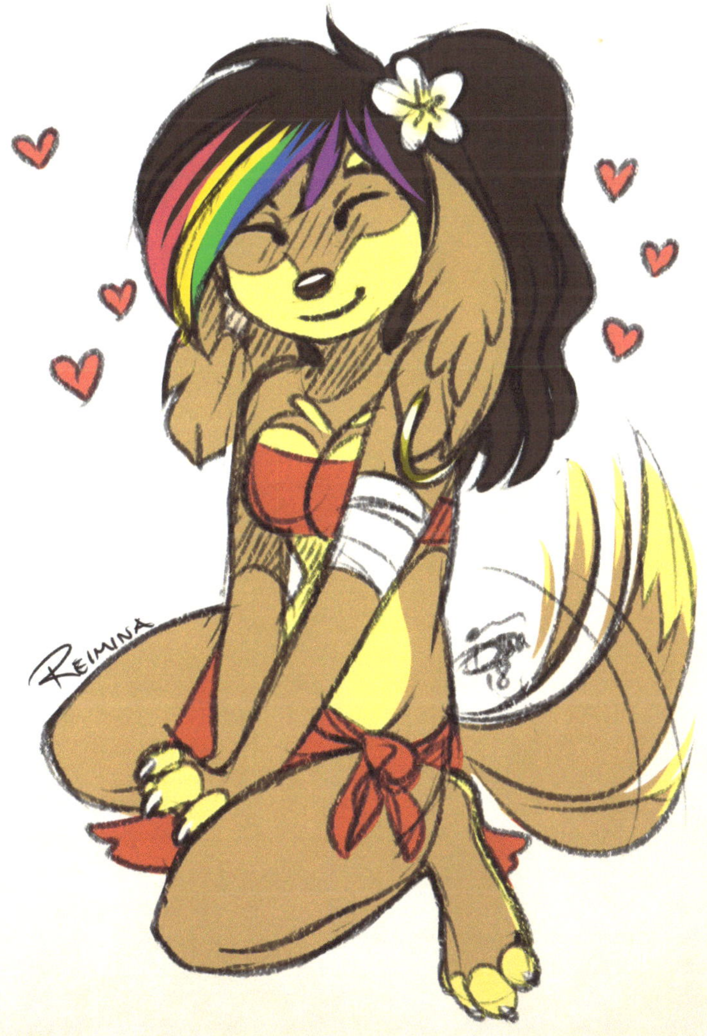

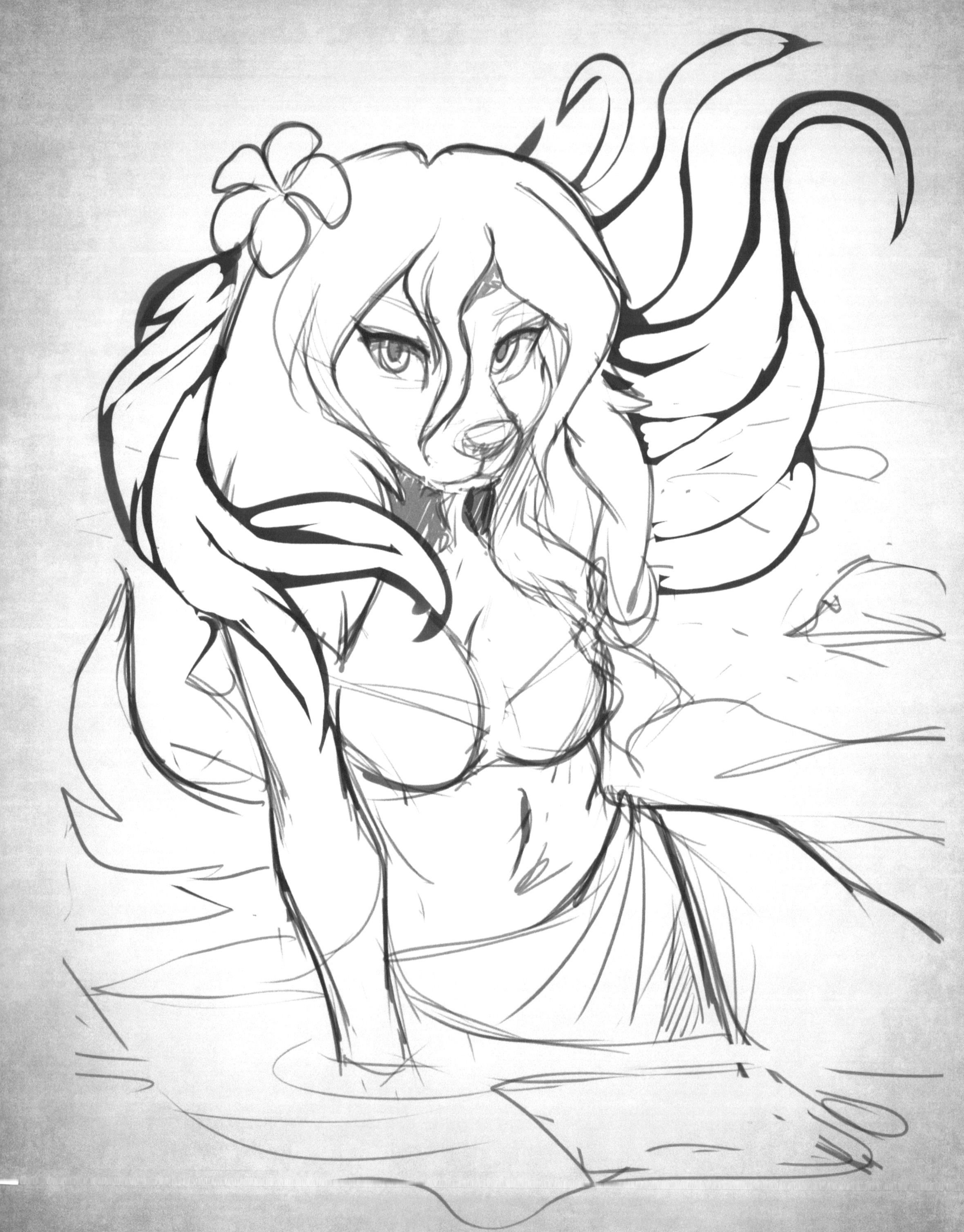

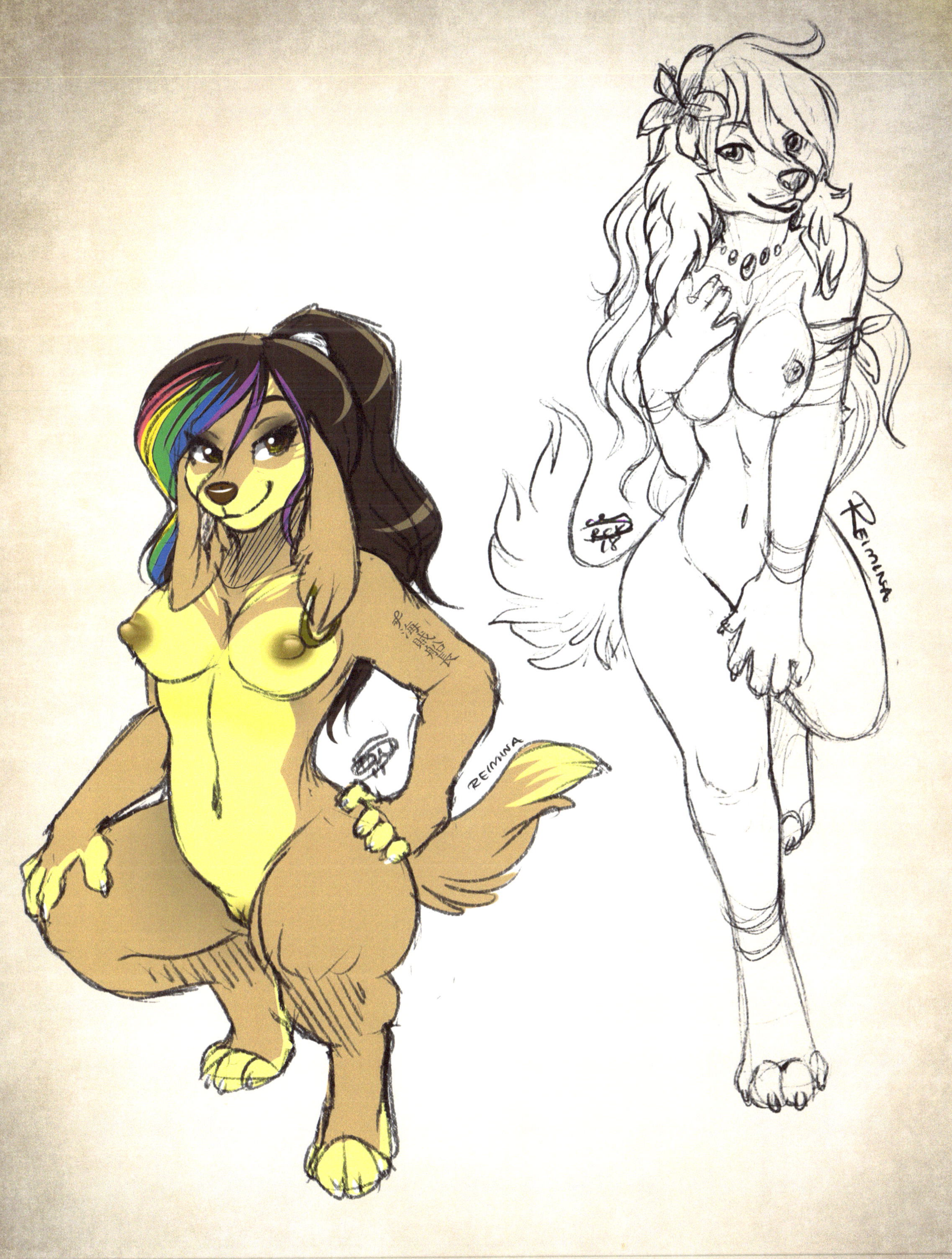
REIMINA
REIMINA

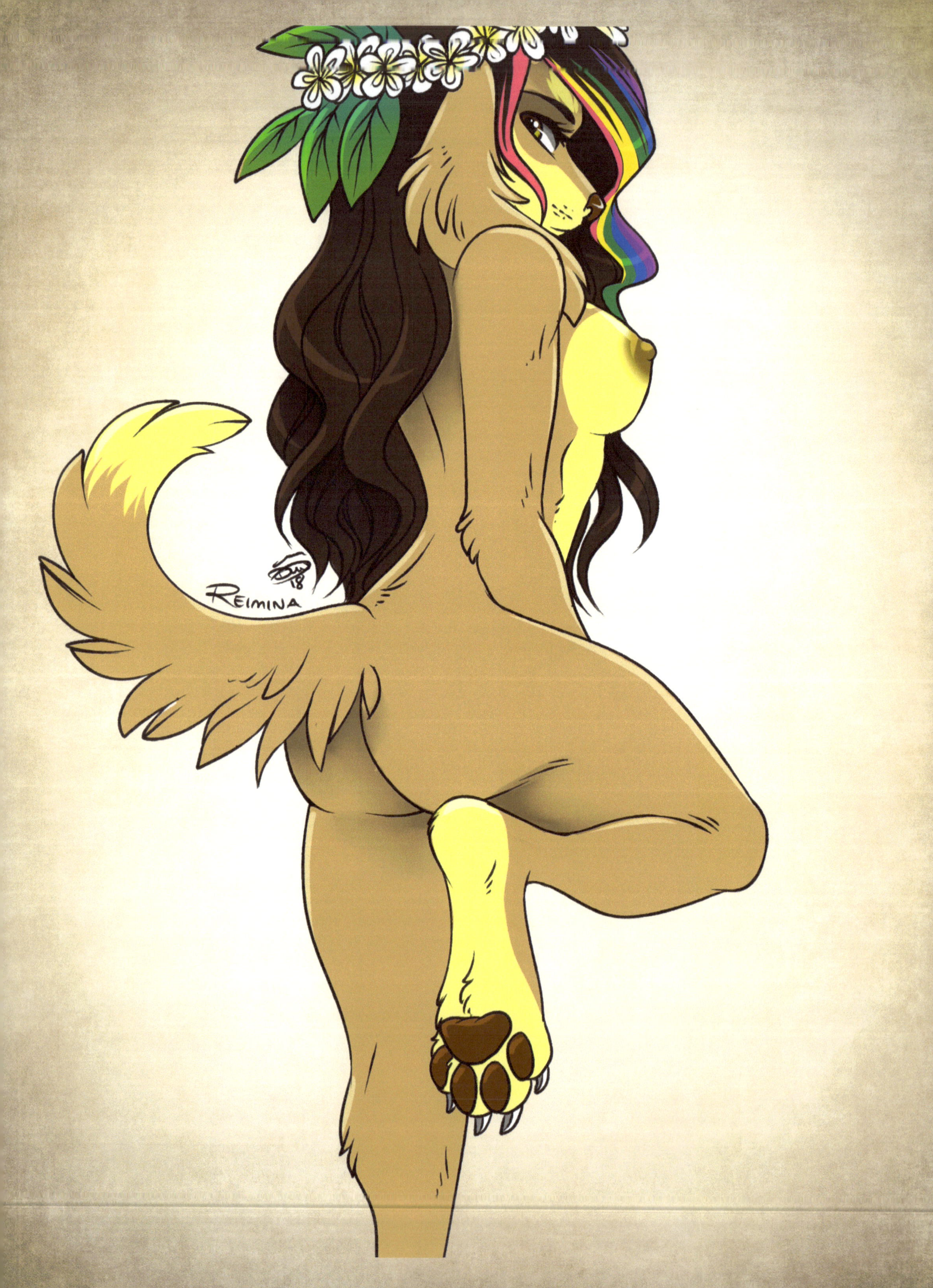
Reimina

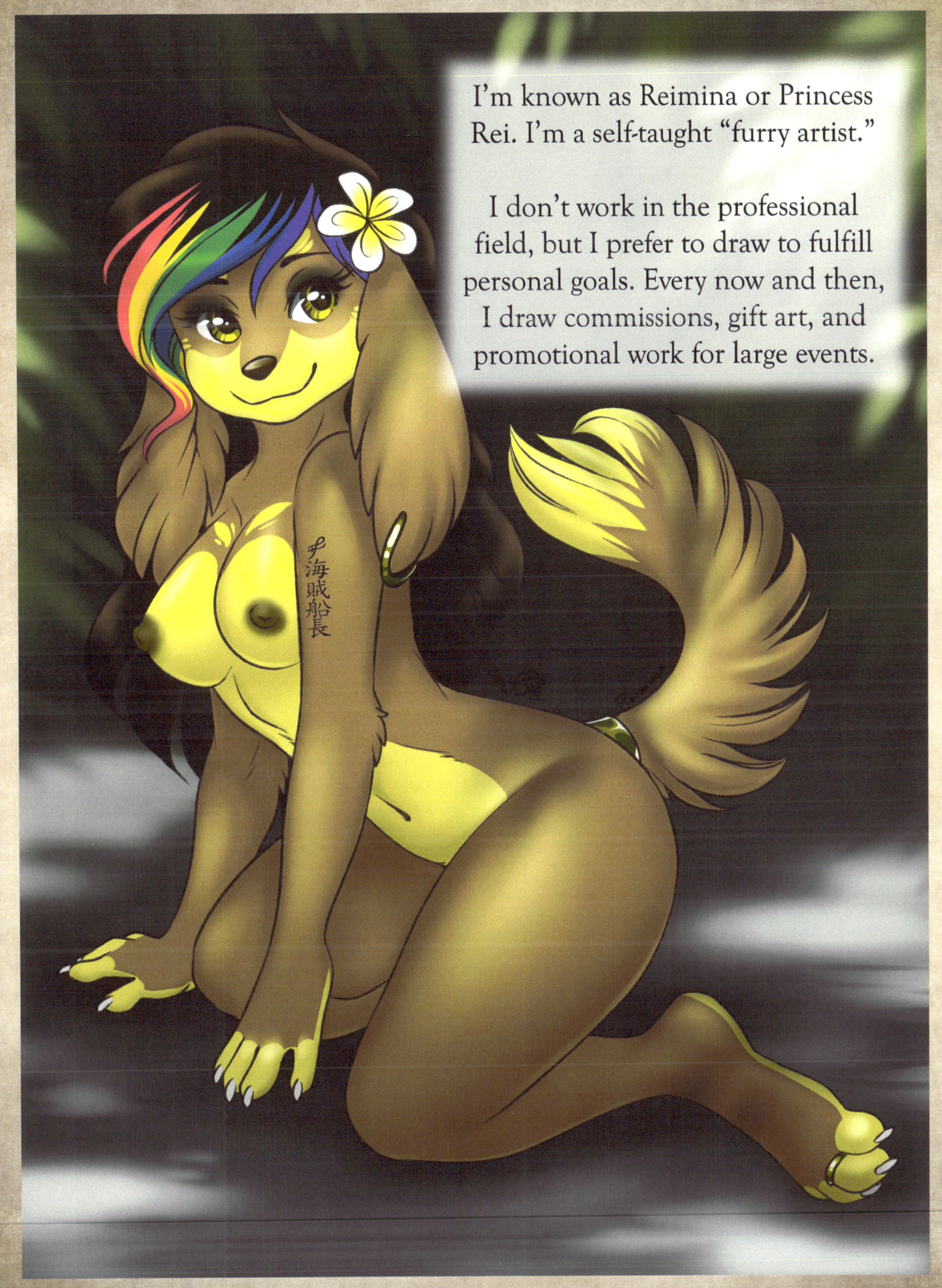
I'm known as Reimina or Princess Rei. I'm a self-taught "furry artist."
I don't work in the professional field, but I prefer to draw to fulfill personal goals. Every now and then, I draw commissions, gift art, and promotional work for large events.
海賊船長

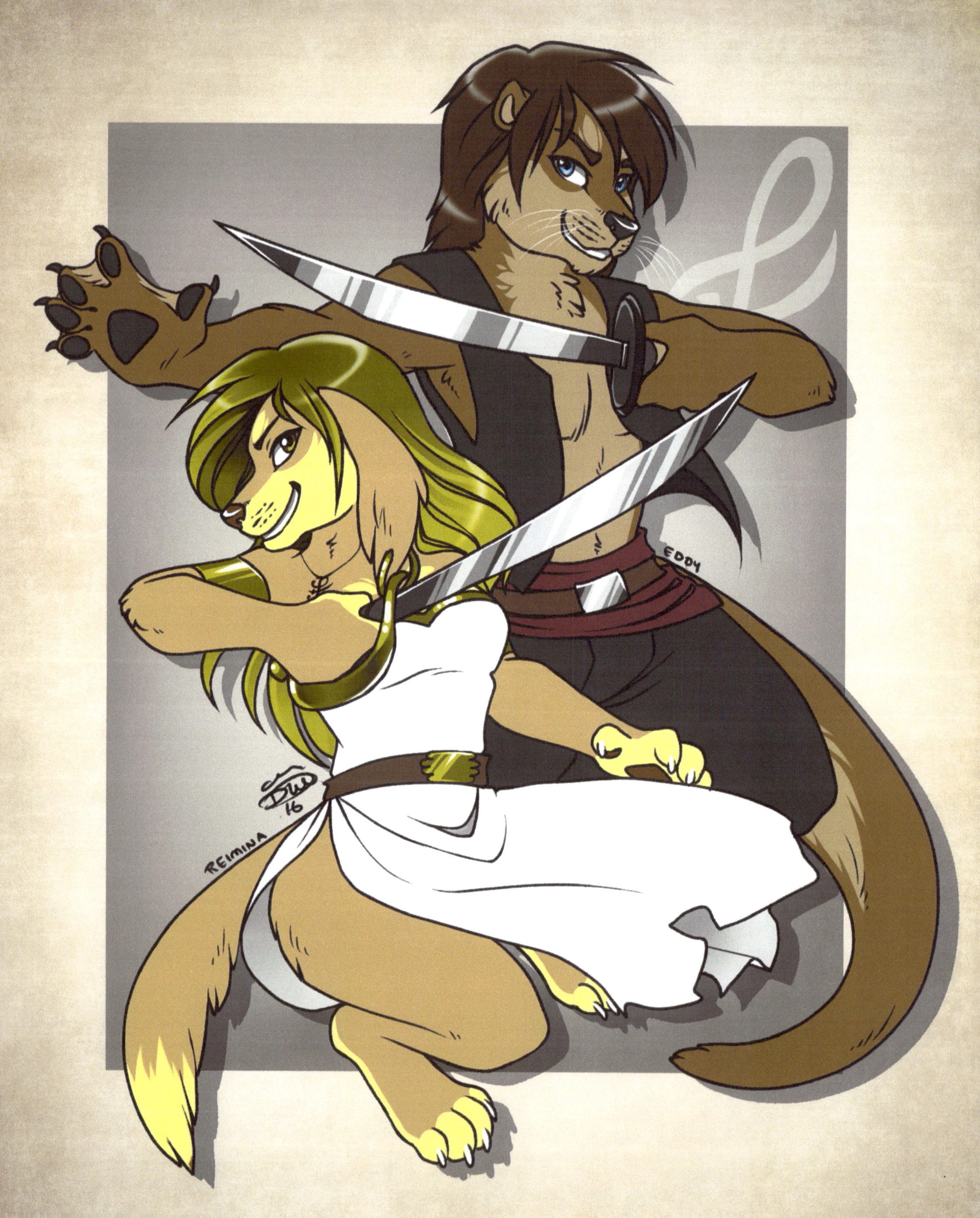
EDDY
REIMINA

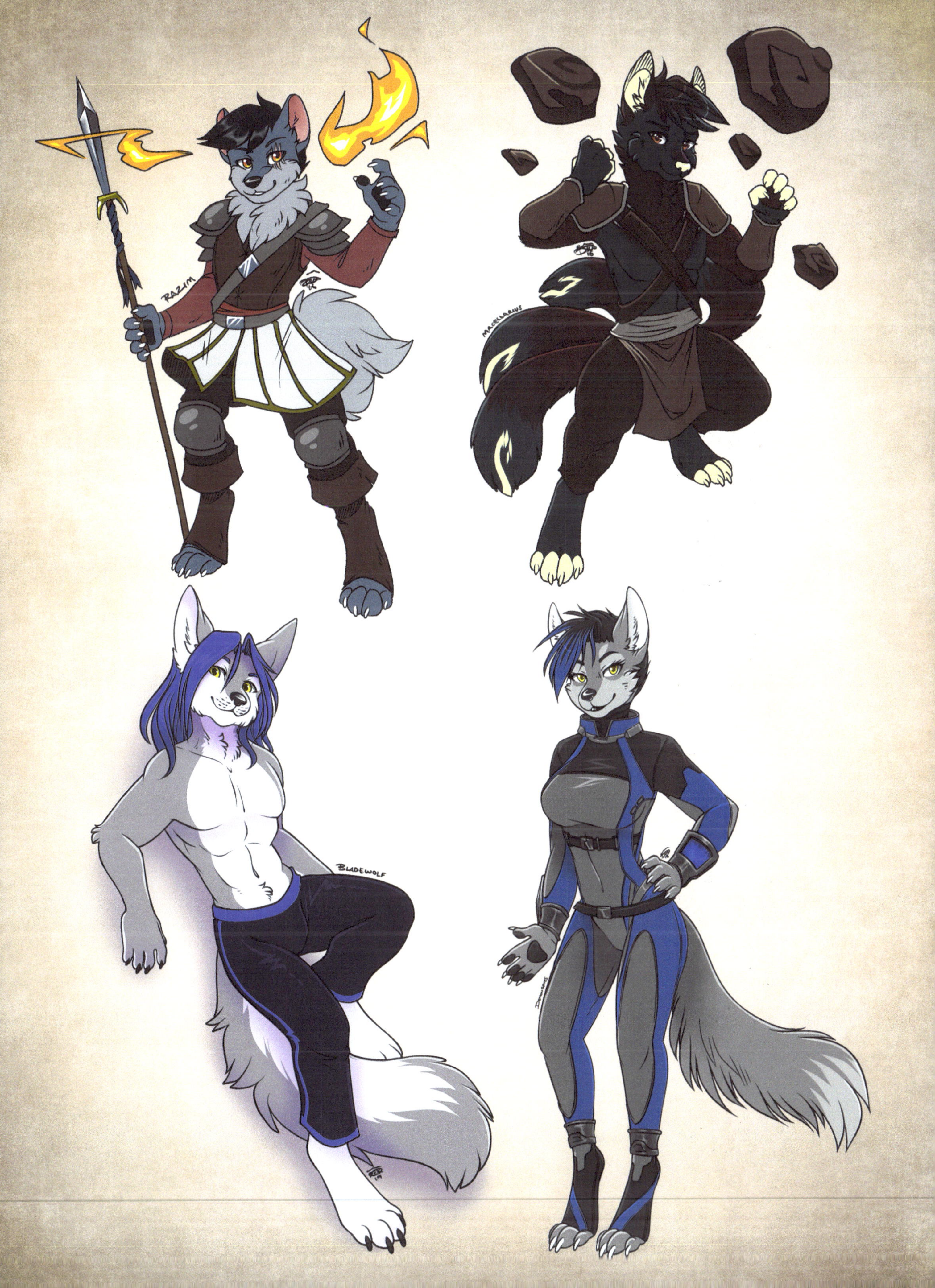
RAZIM
MACELLARIUS
BLADEWOLF

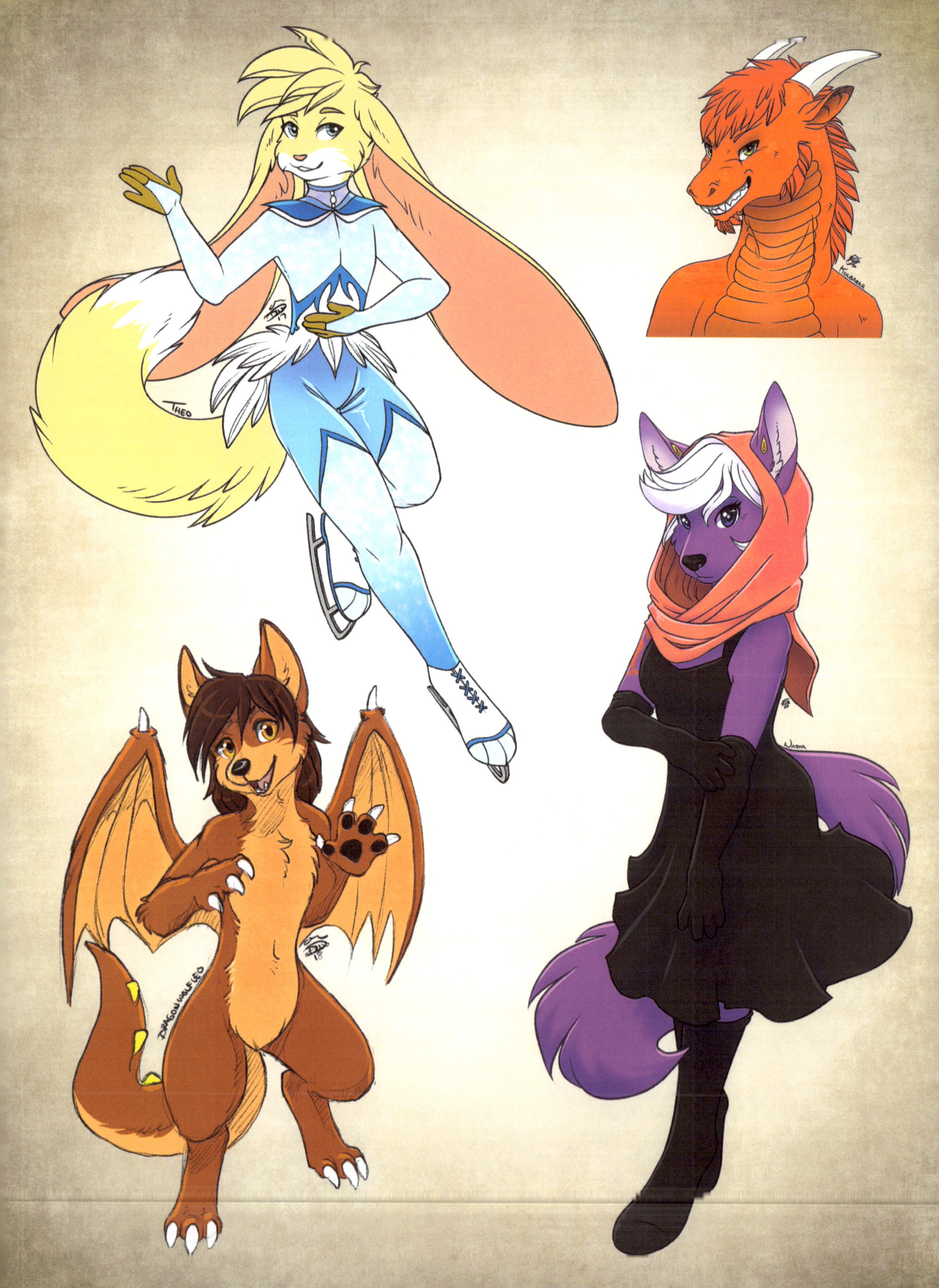
THEO
KULBARAH
NADIA
DRAGONWOLFLEO

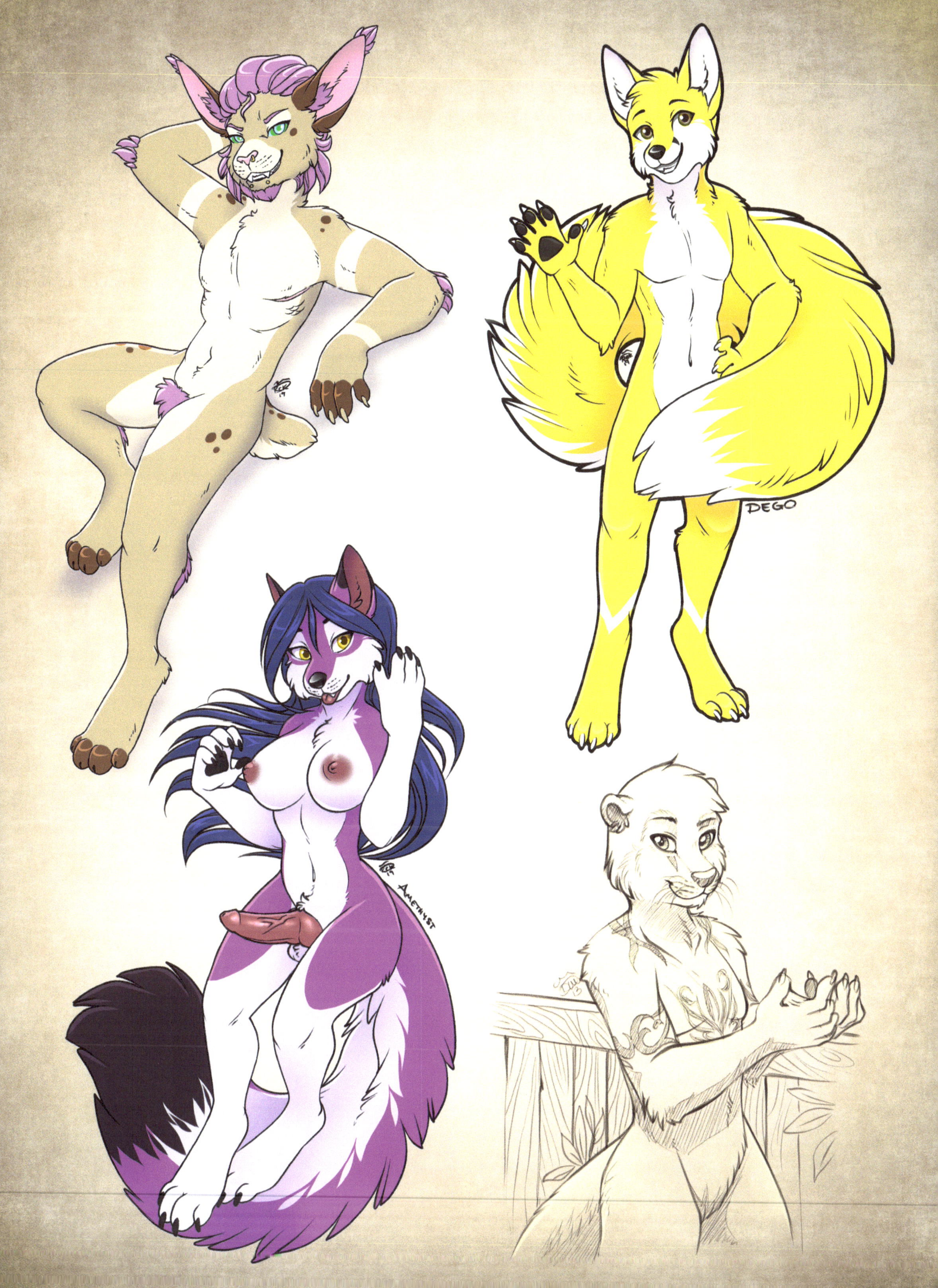
DEGO
Amethyst

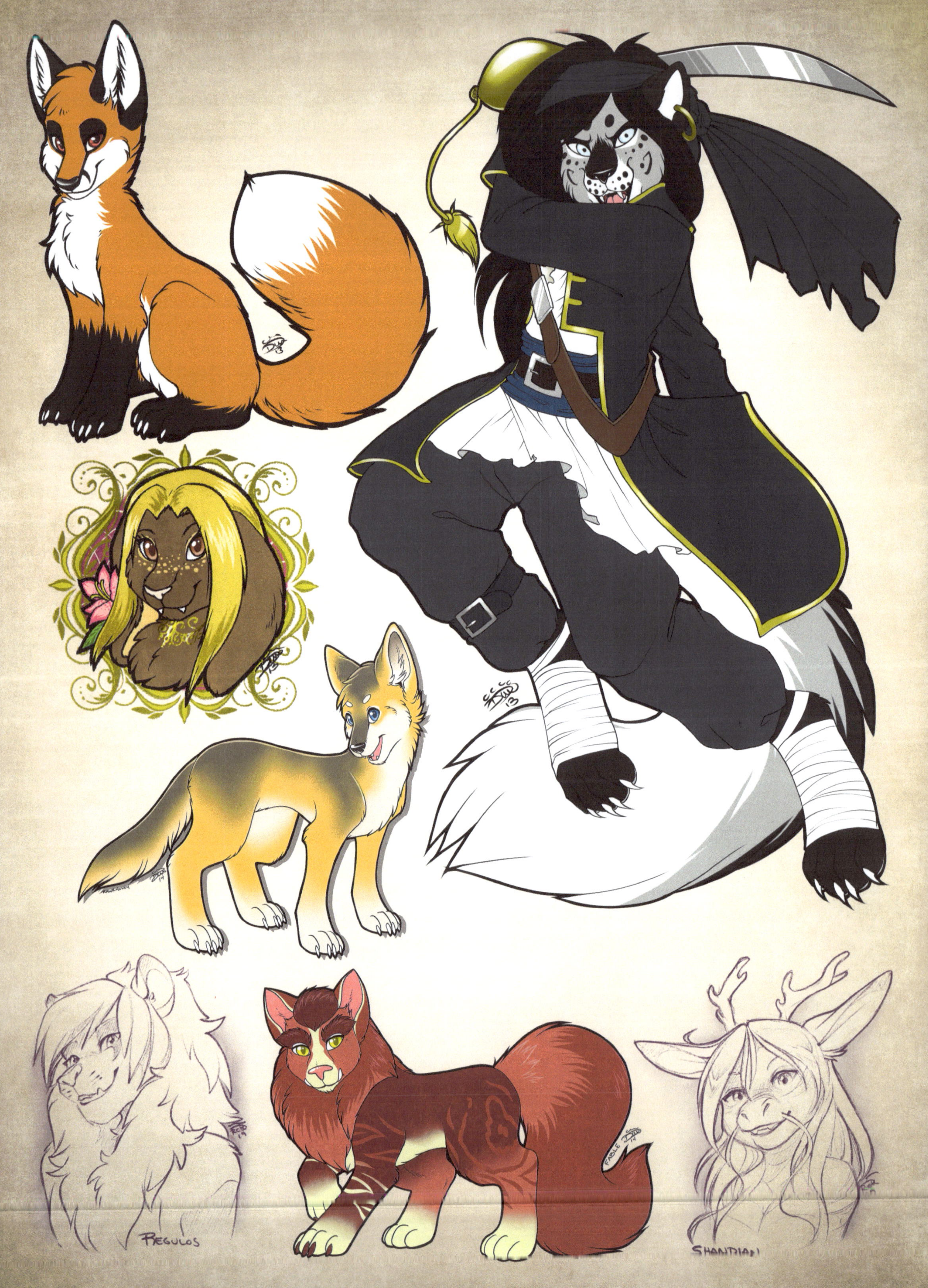
REGULOS
FABLE
SHANDIANI

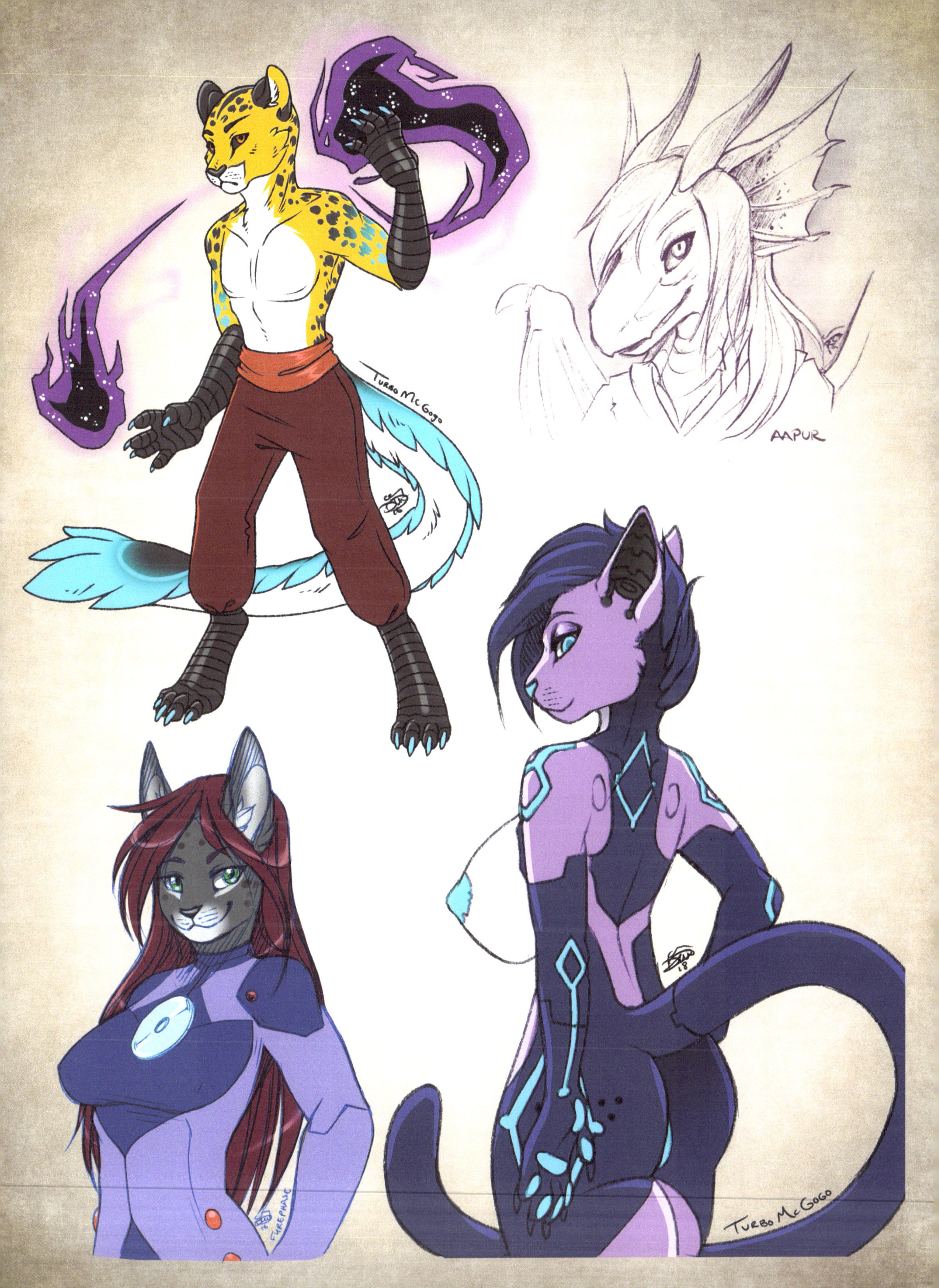
Turbo McGogo
AAPUR
Turbo McGogo

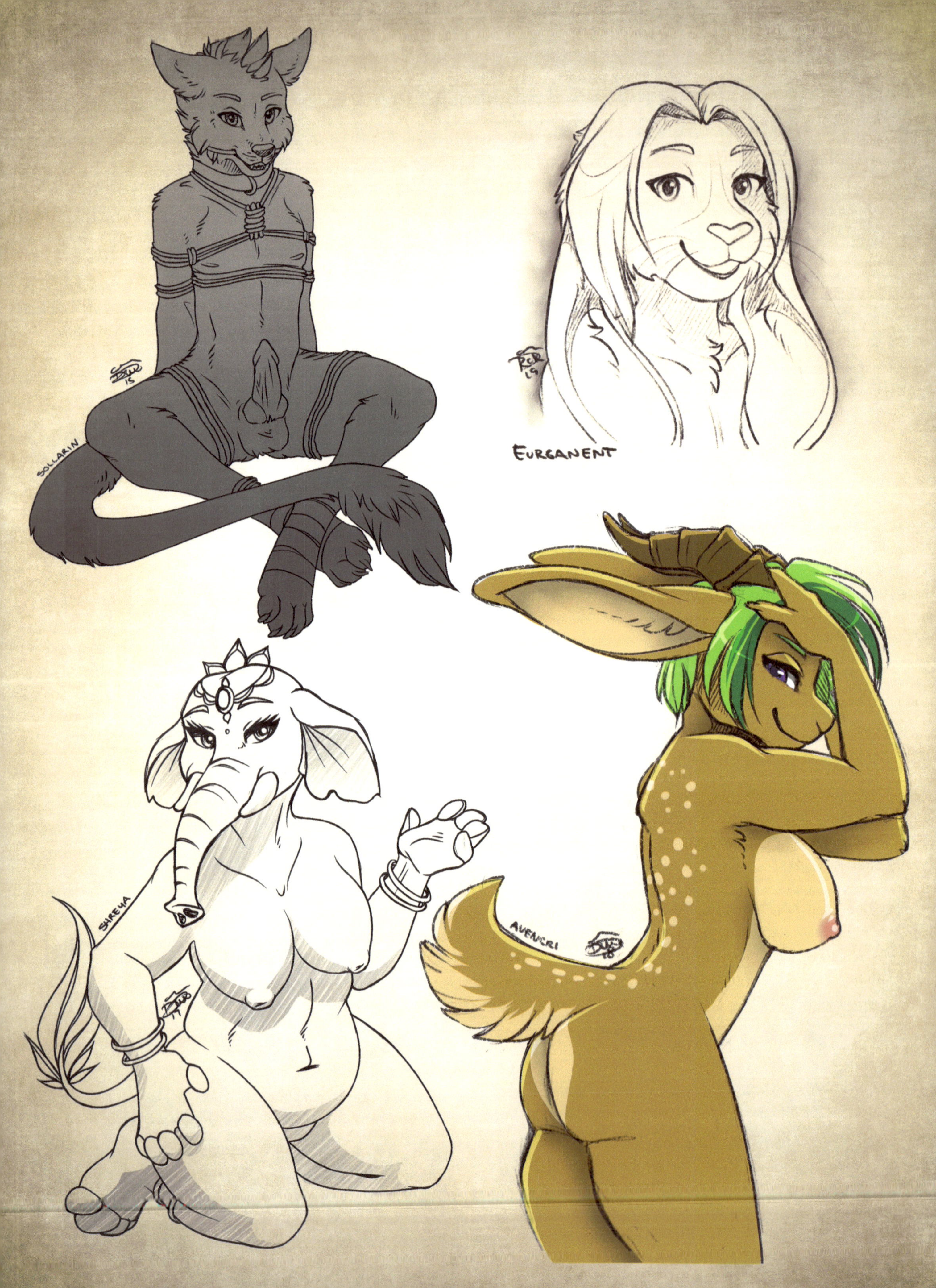
SOLLARIN
EURGANENT
SHREYA
AVENCRI

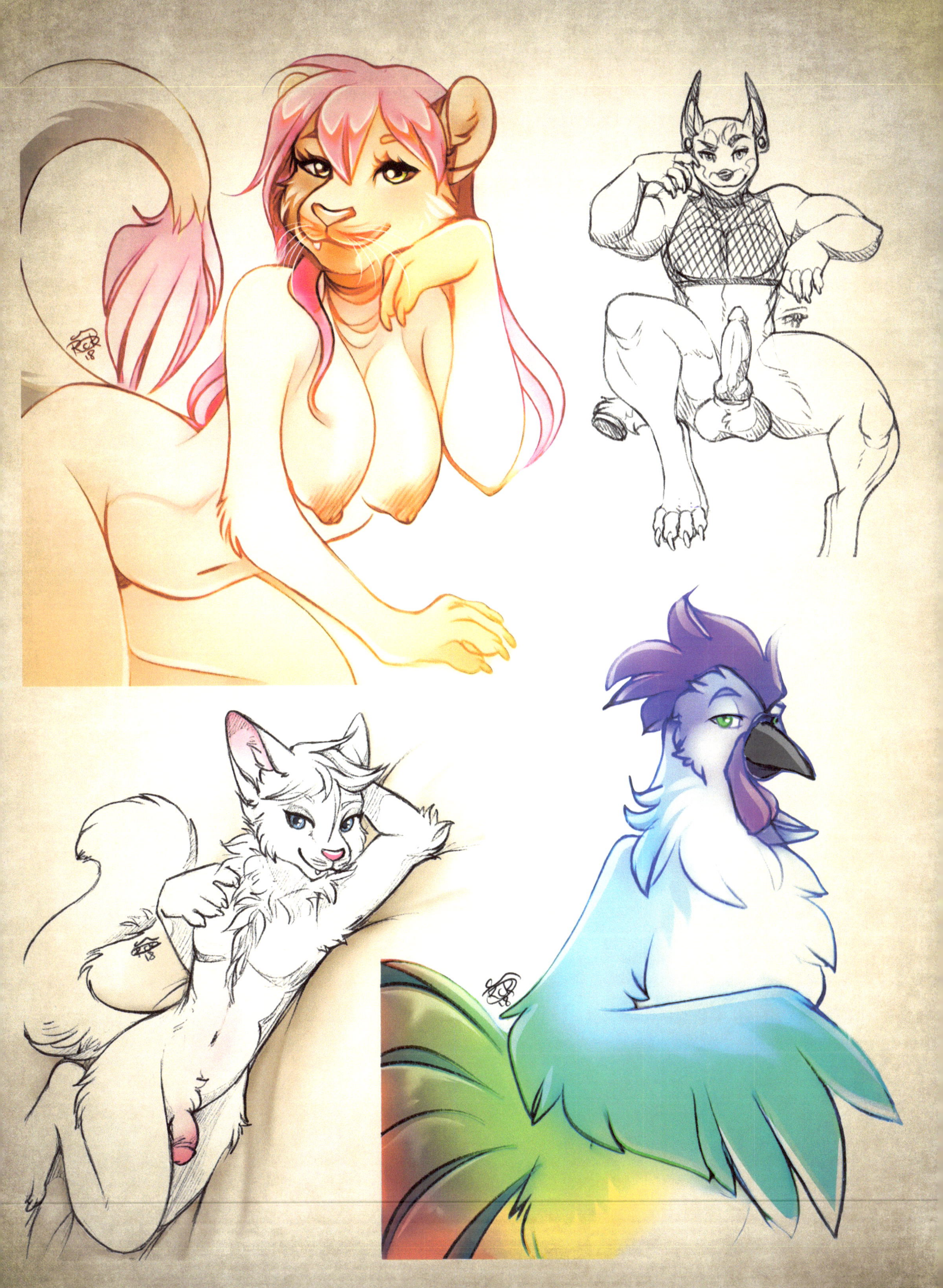

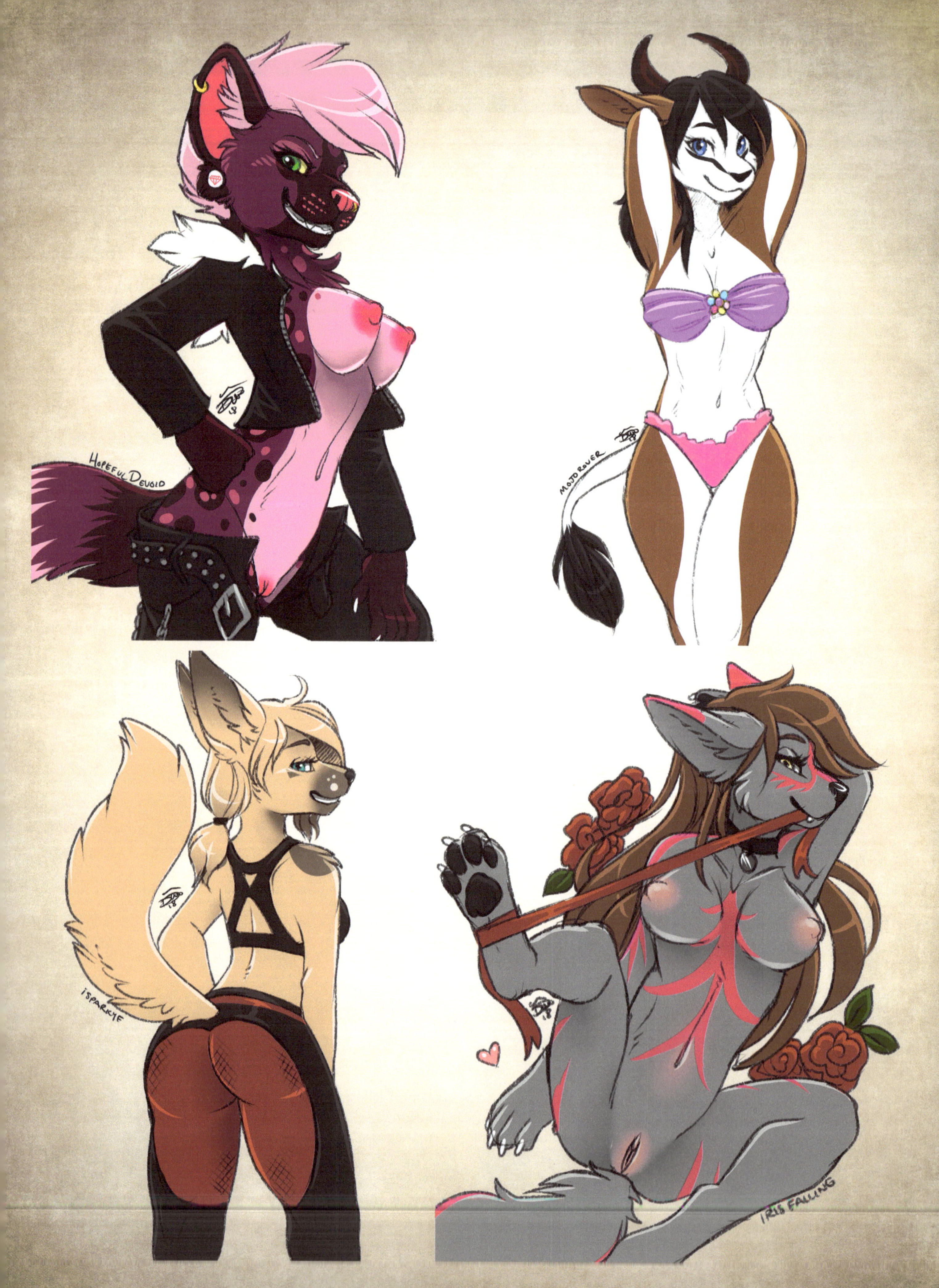
HopefulDevoid
MojoRover
iSparkye
IrisFalling

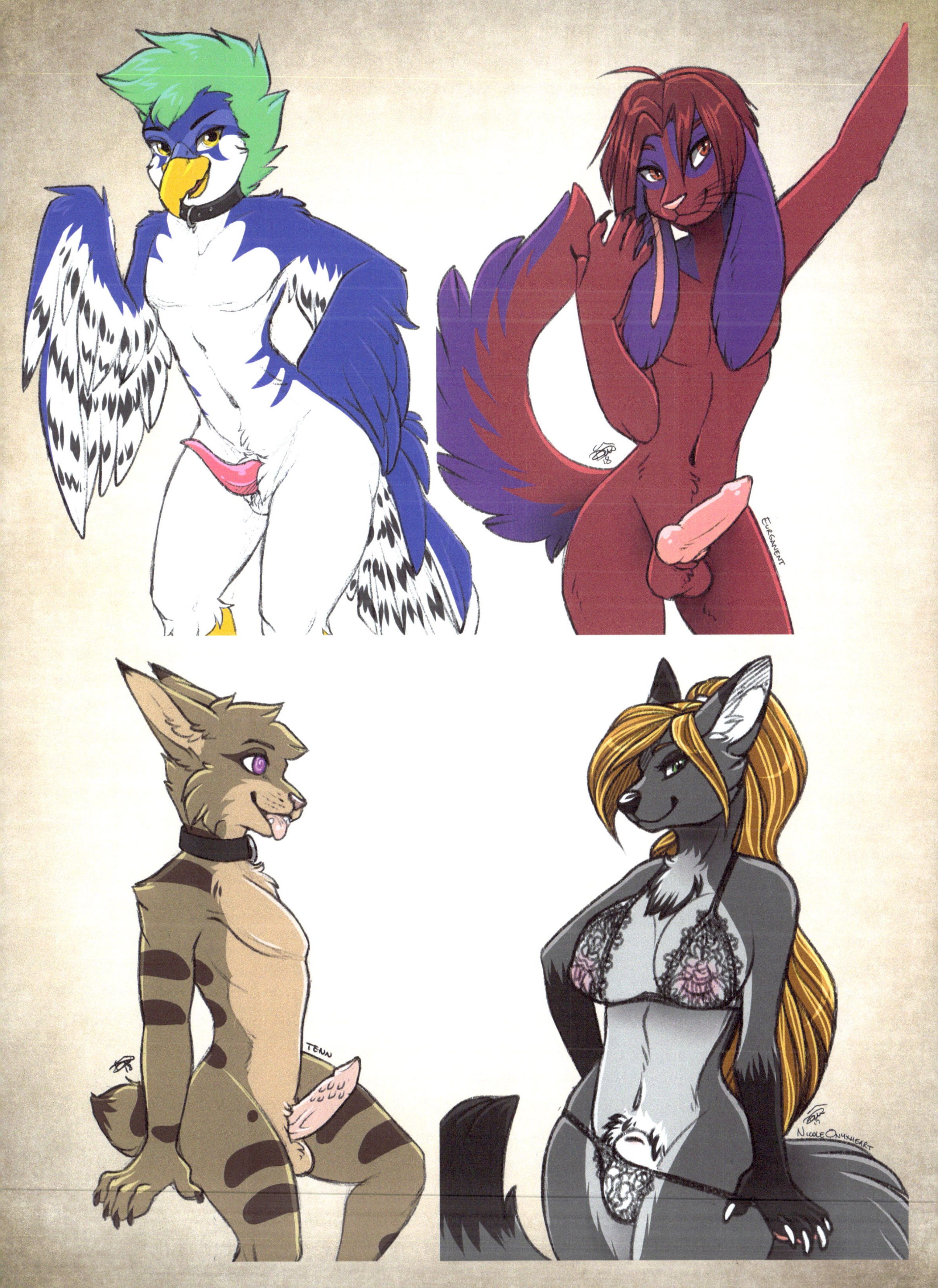
EURGANENT
TENN
NICOLEONYXHEART

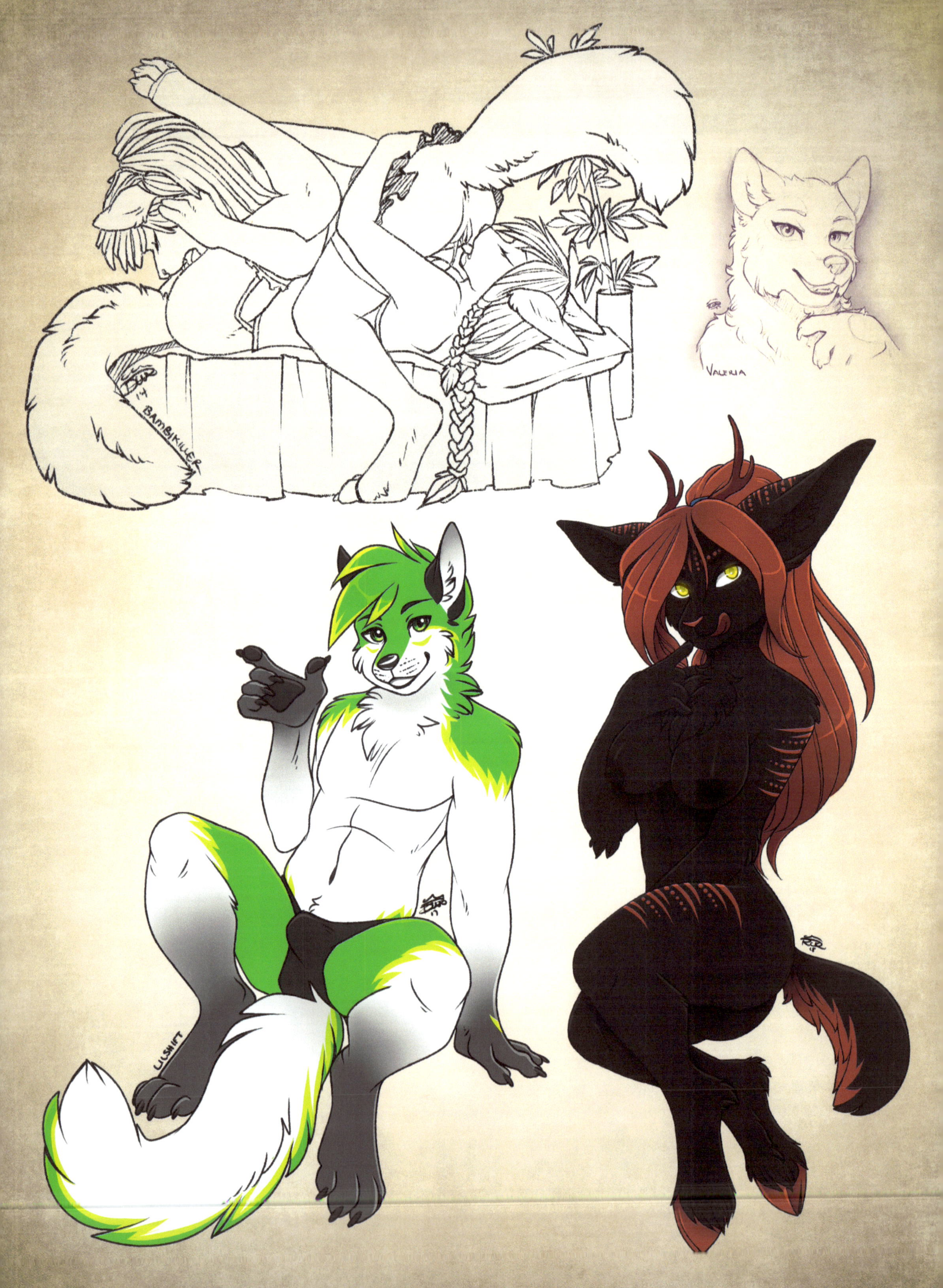
BAMBIKILLER
VALERIA
LILSHIFT

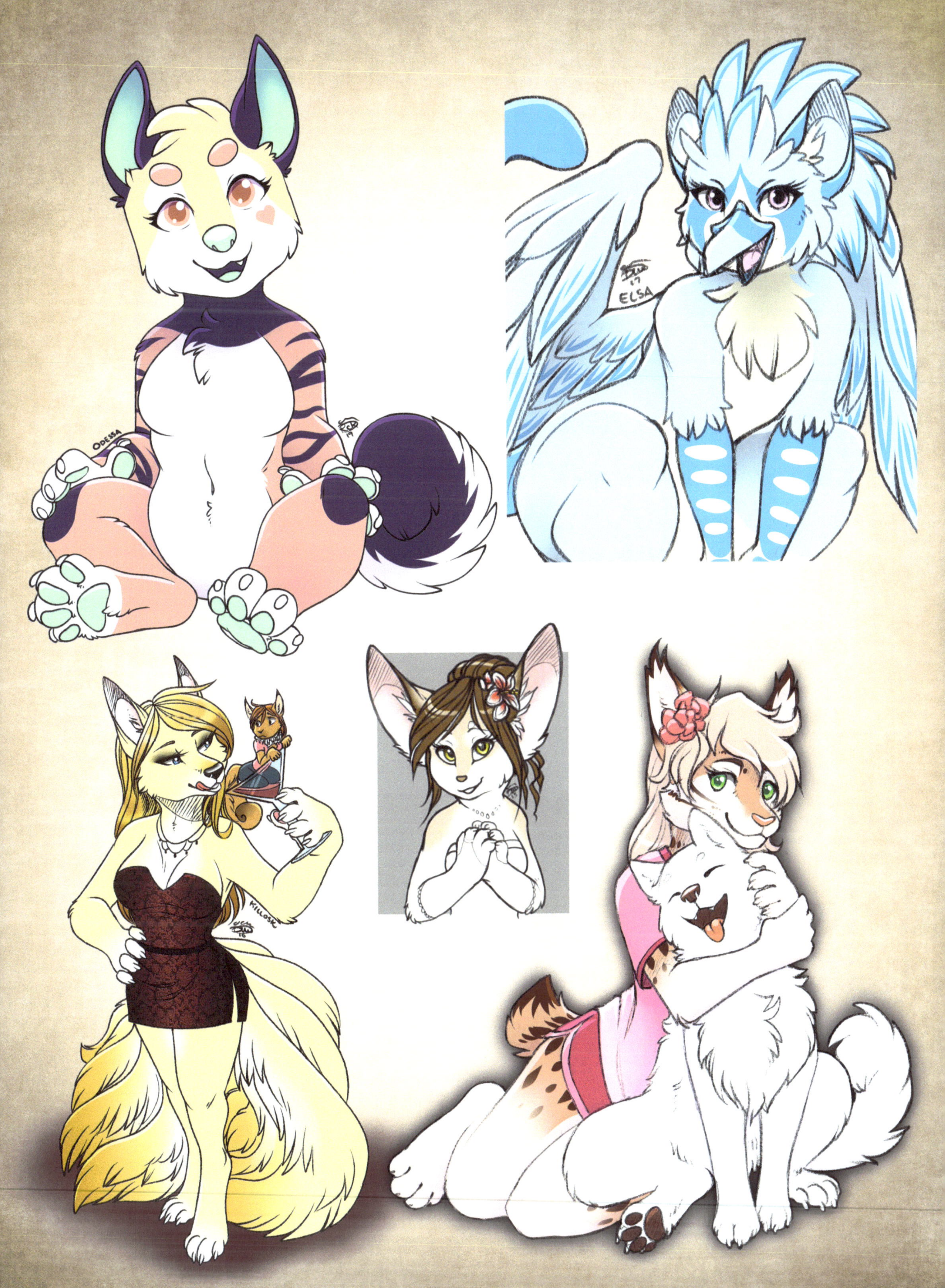
ODESSA
ELSA
KILLOSK

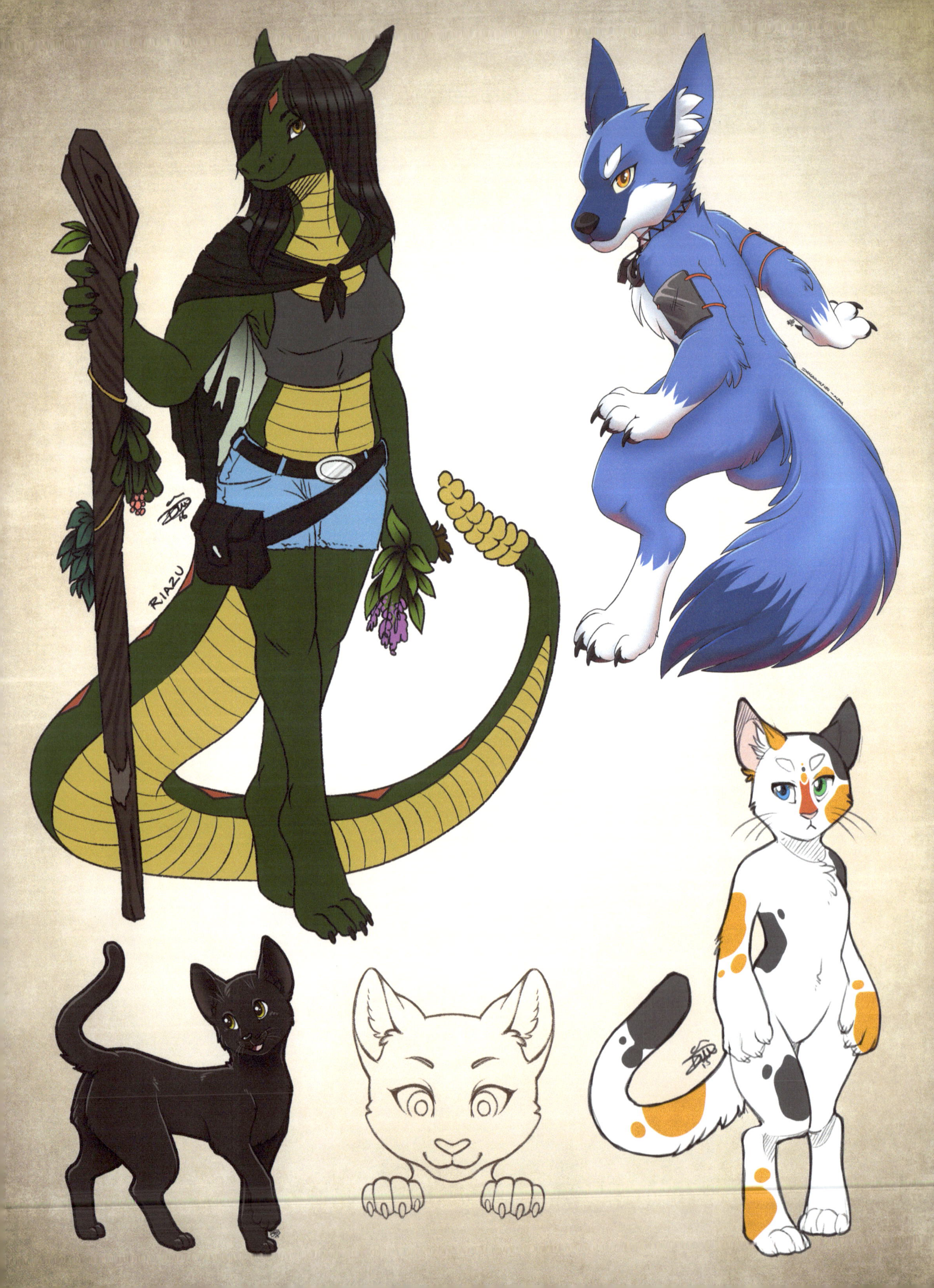
RIAZU

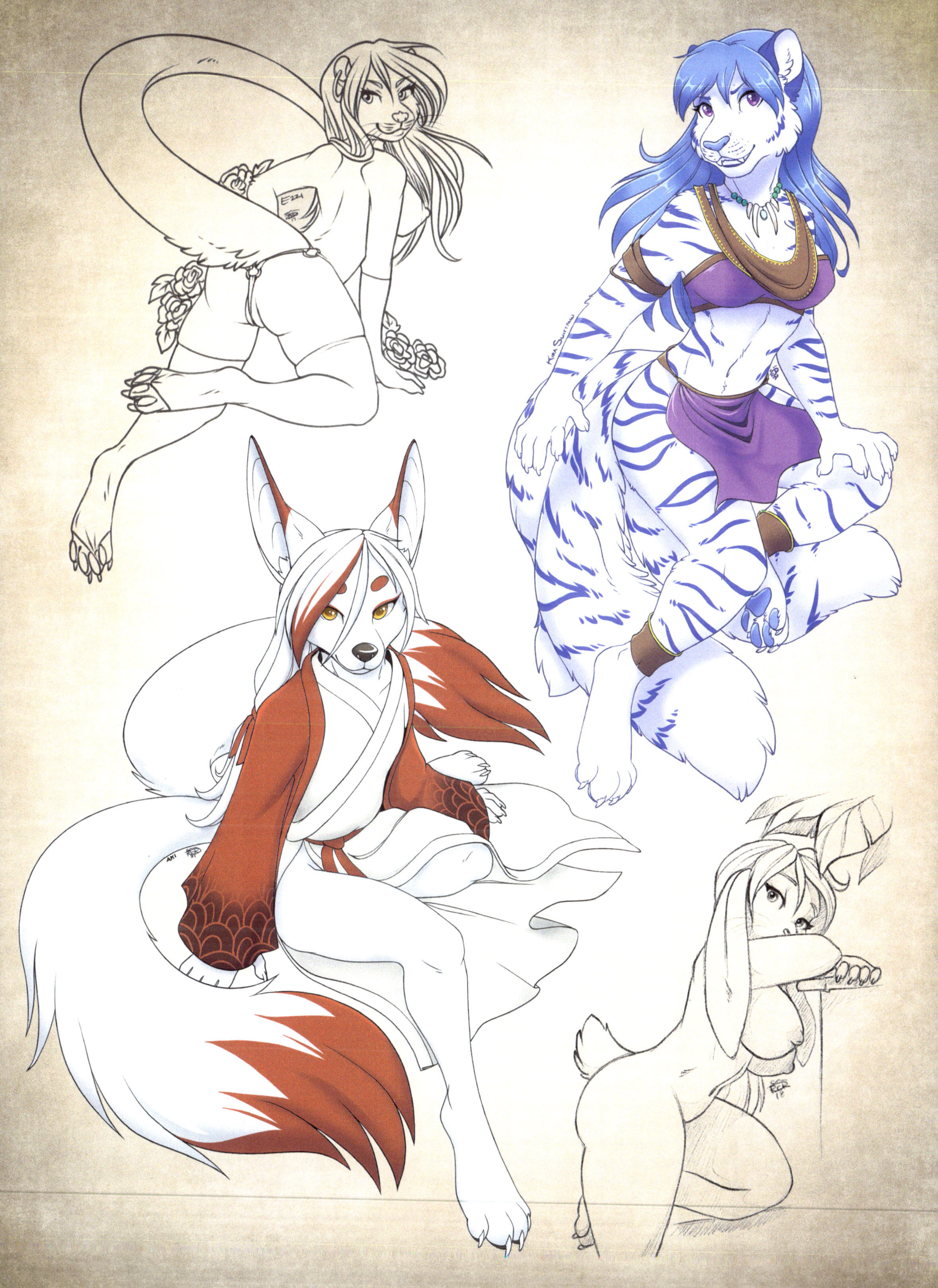

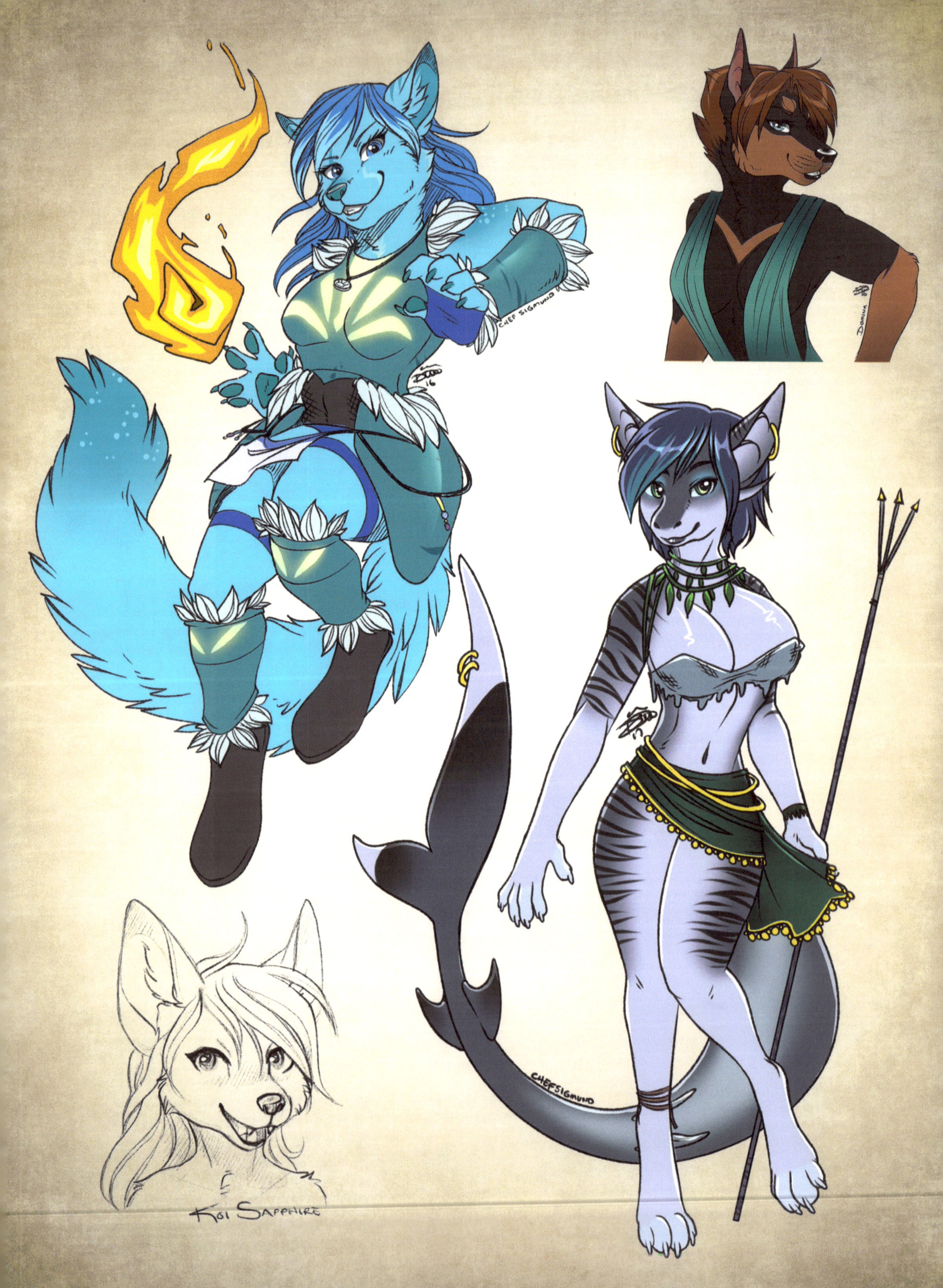
CHEF SIGMUND
DOMINA
CHEFSIGMUND
KOI SAPPHIRE

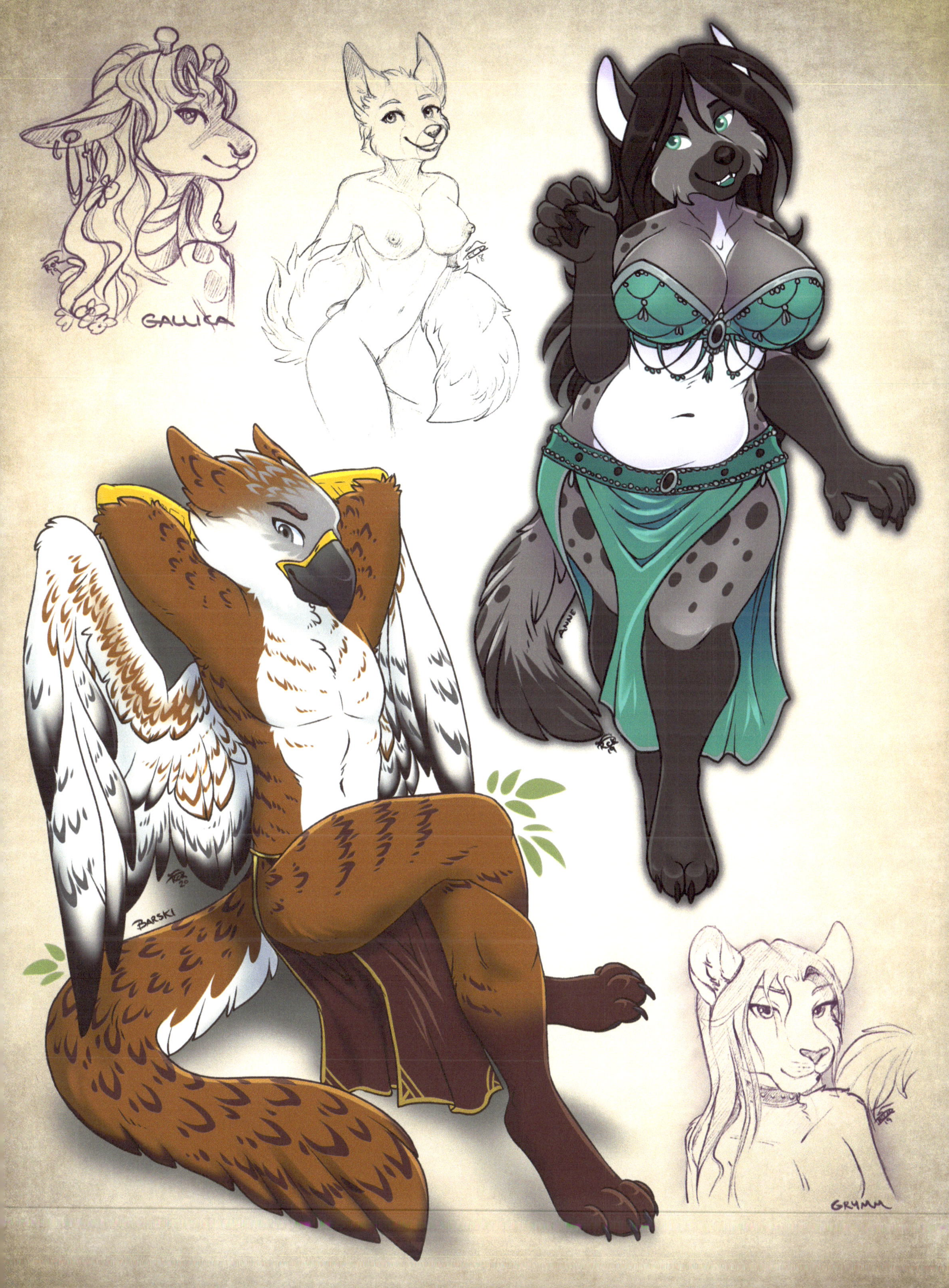
GALLICA
ANNE
BARSKI
GRYMM

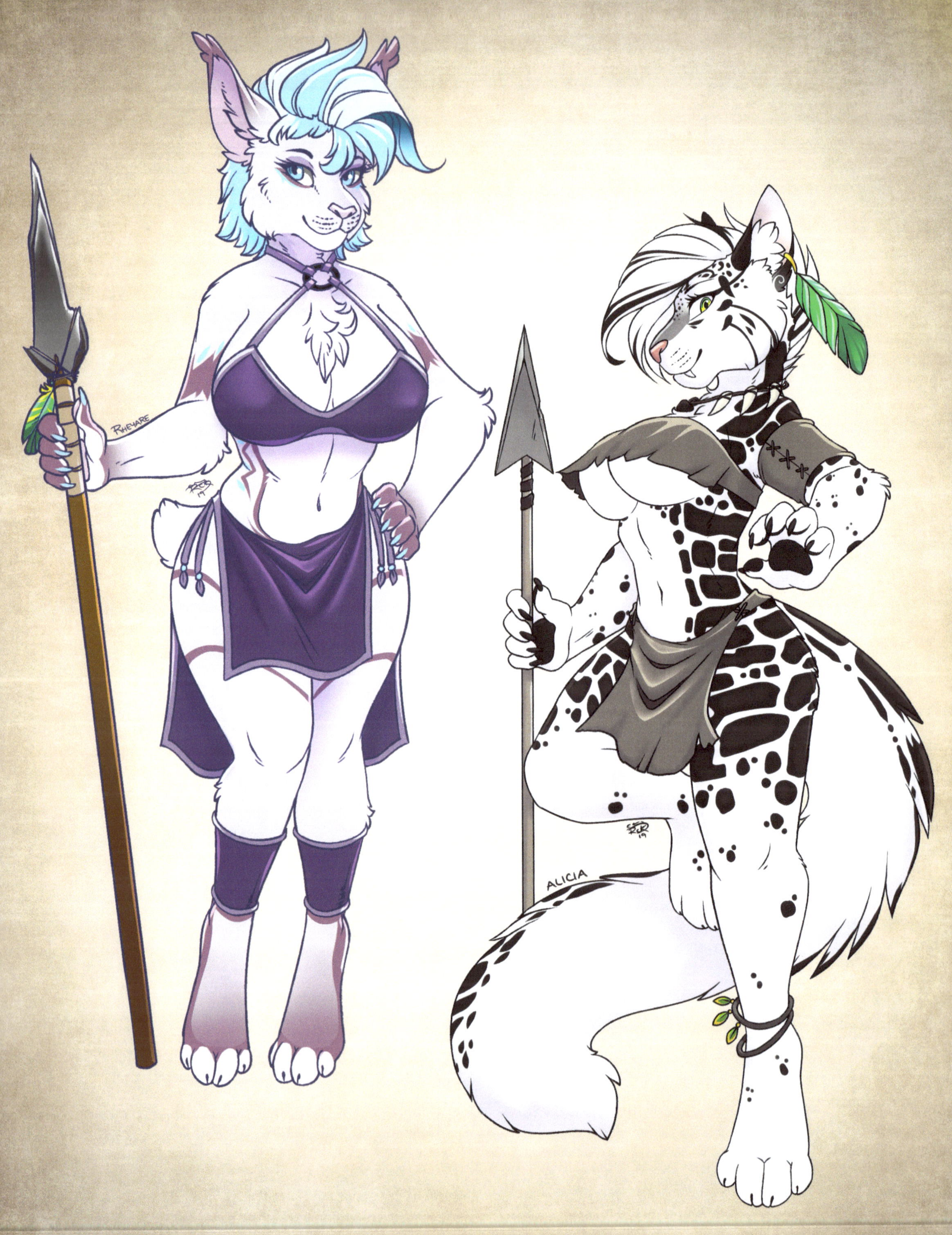
RHEYARE
ALICIA

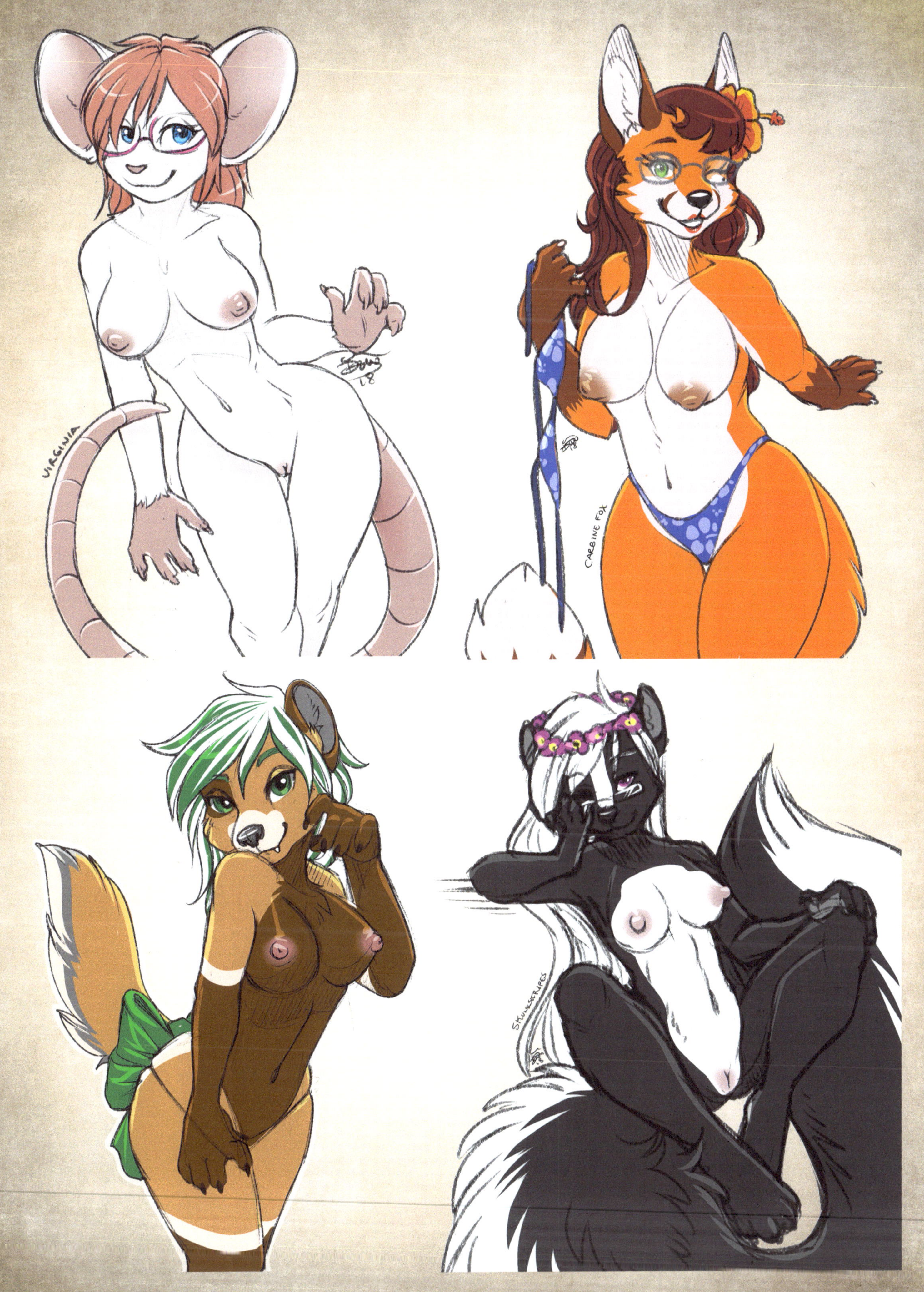
VIRGINIA
CARBINE FOX
SKUNKSTRIPES

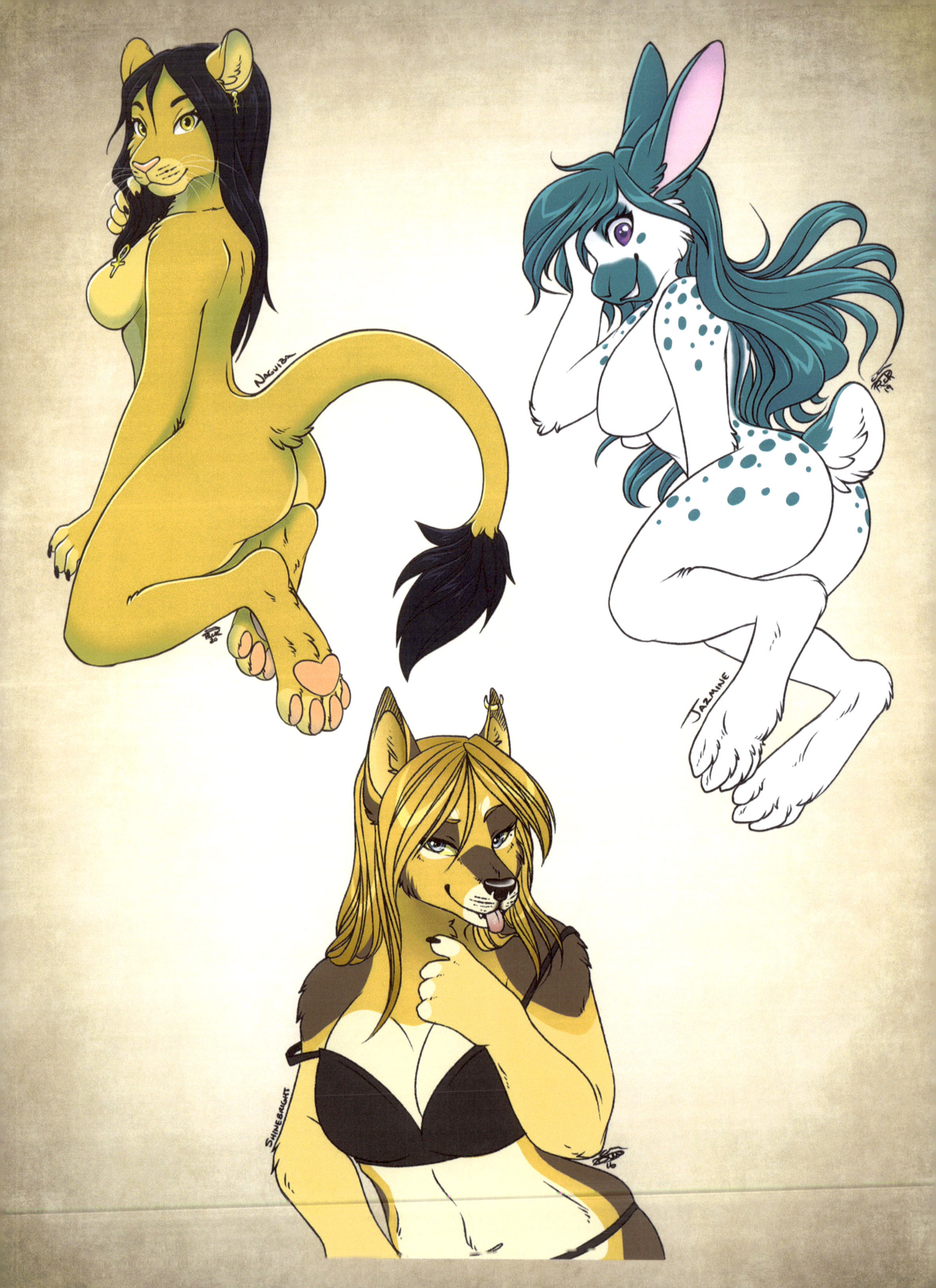
Naguiba
Jazmine
Shinebright

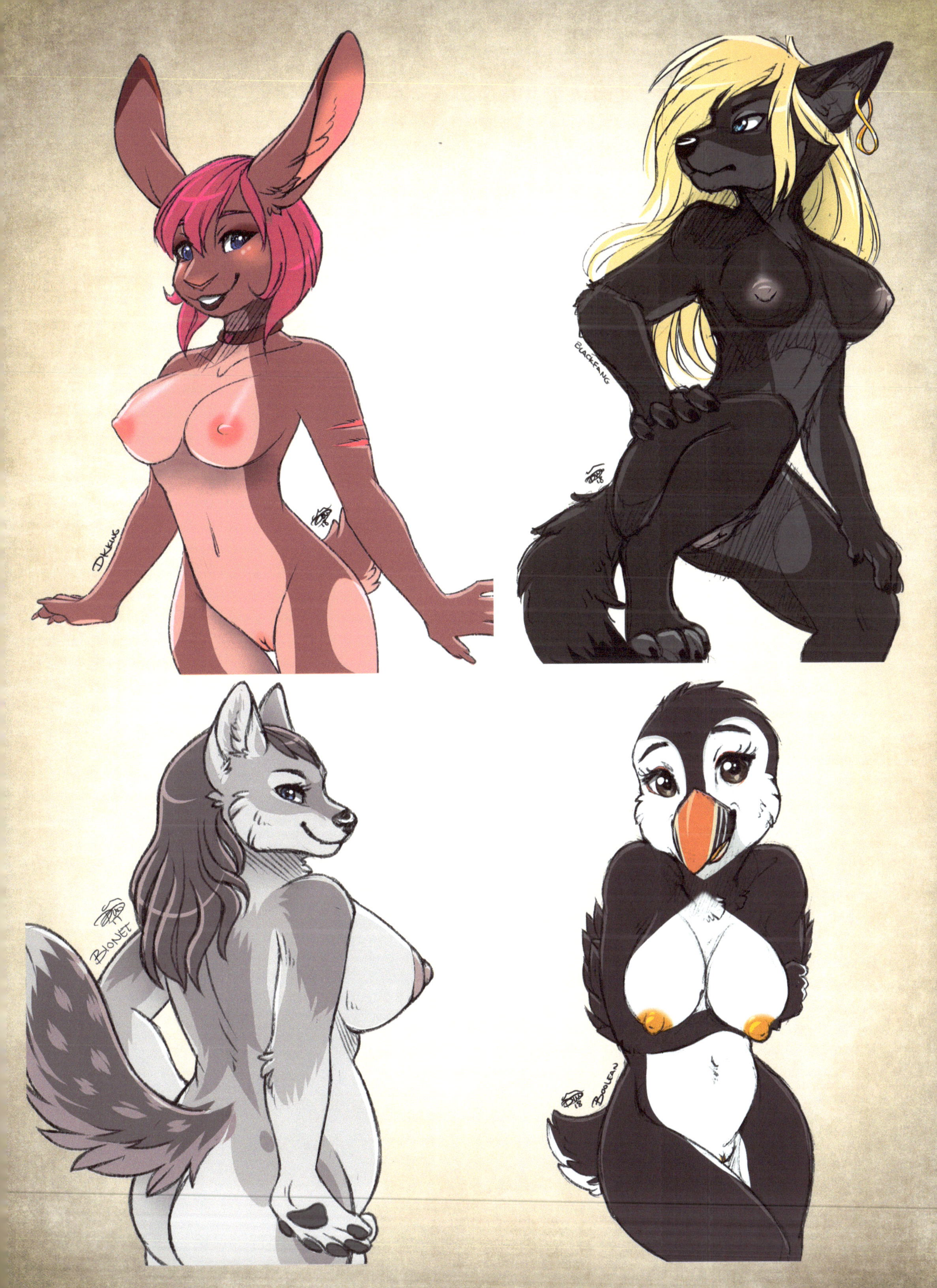
DKKING
BLACKFANG
BIONET
BOOLEAN

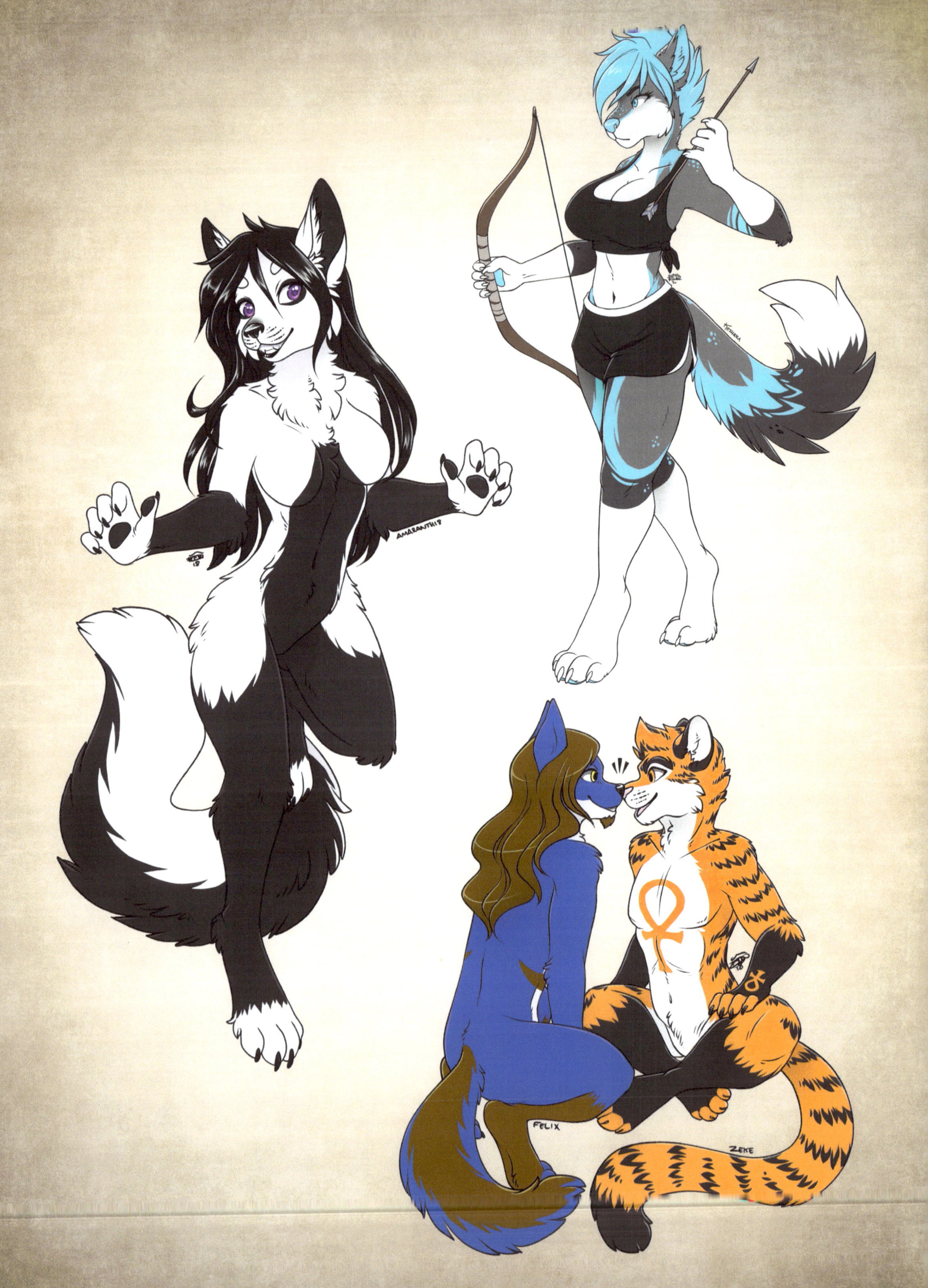
AMARANTH18
KESHARA
FELIX
ZEKE

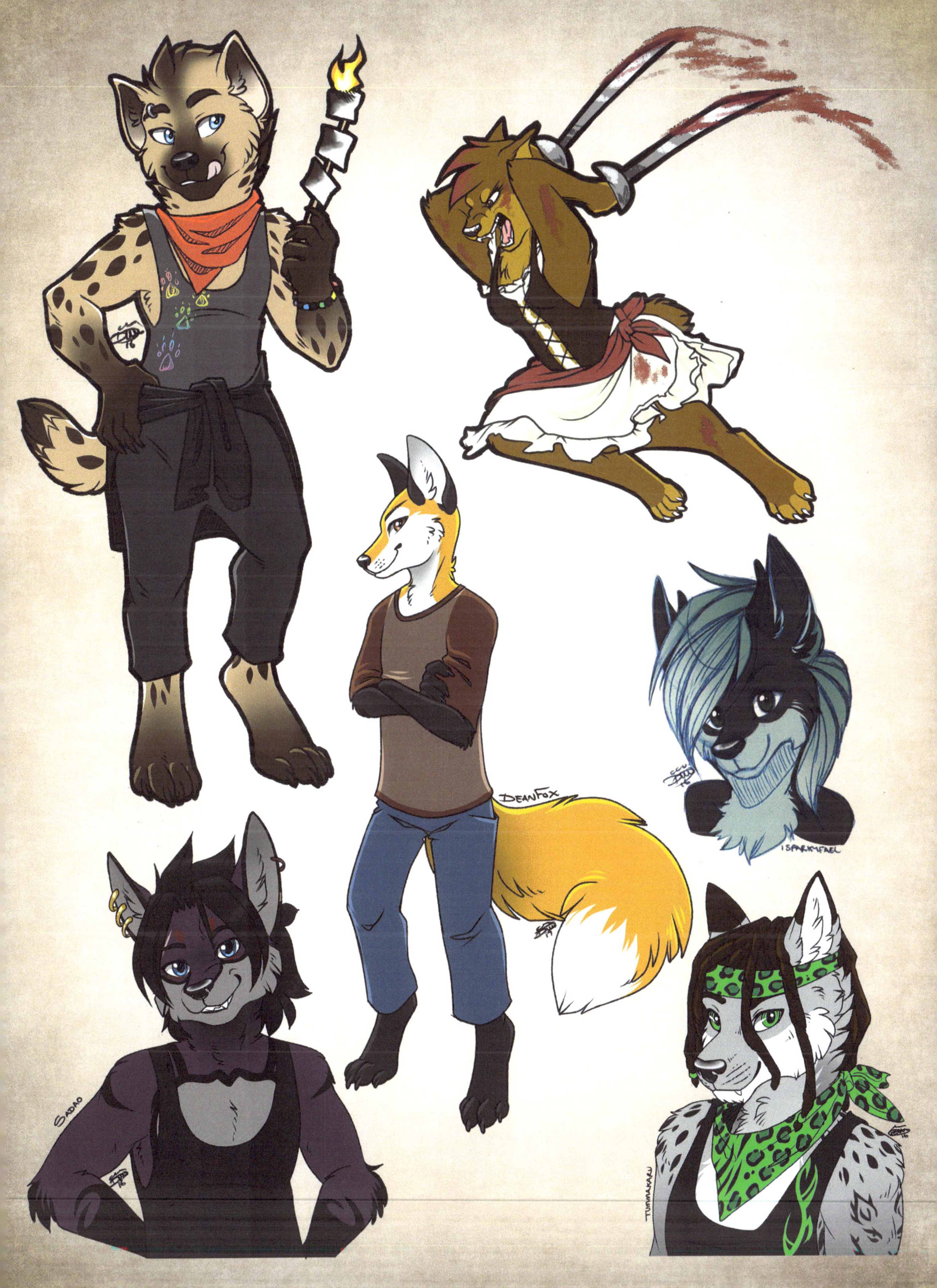
DeanFox
iSparkyFael
Sadao
Tummakaru

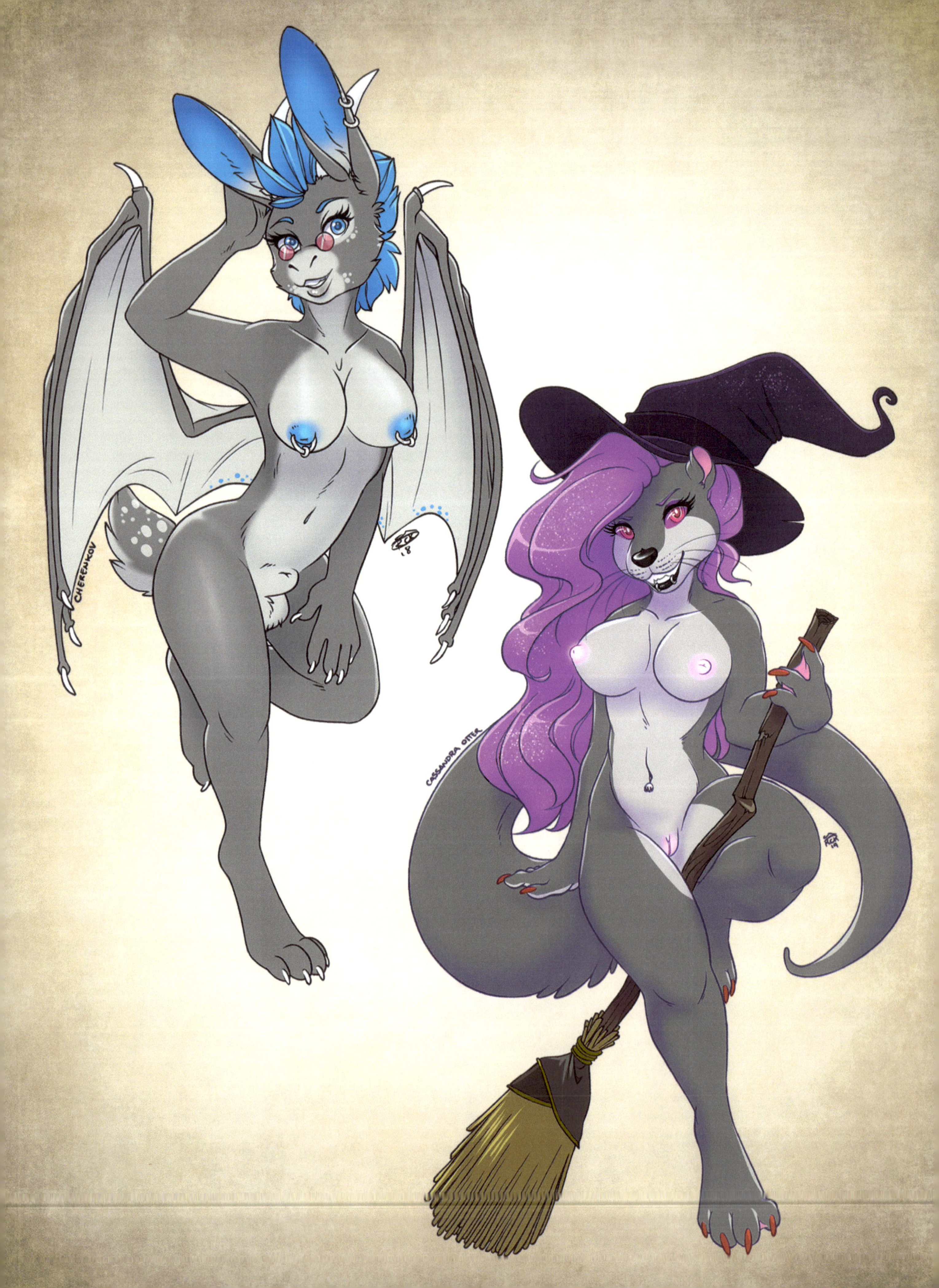
CHERENKOV
CASSANDRA OTTER

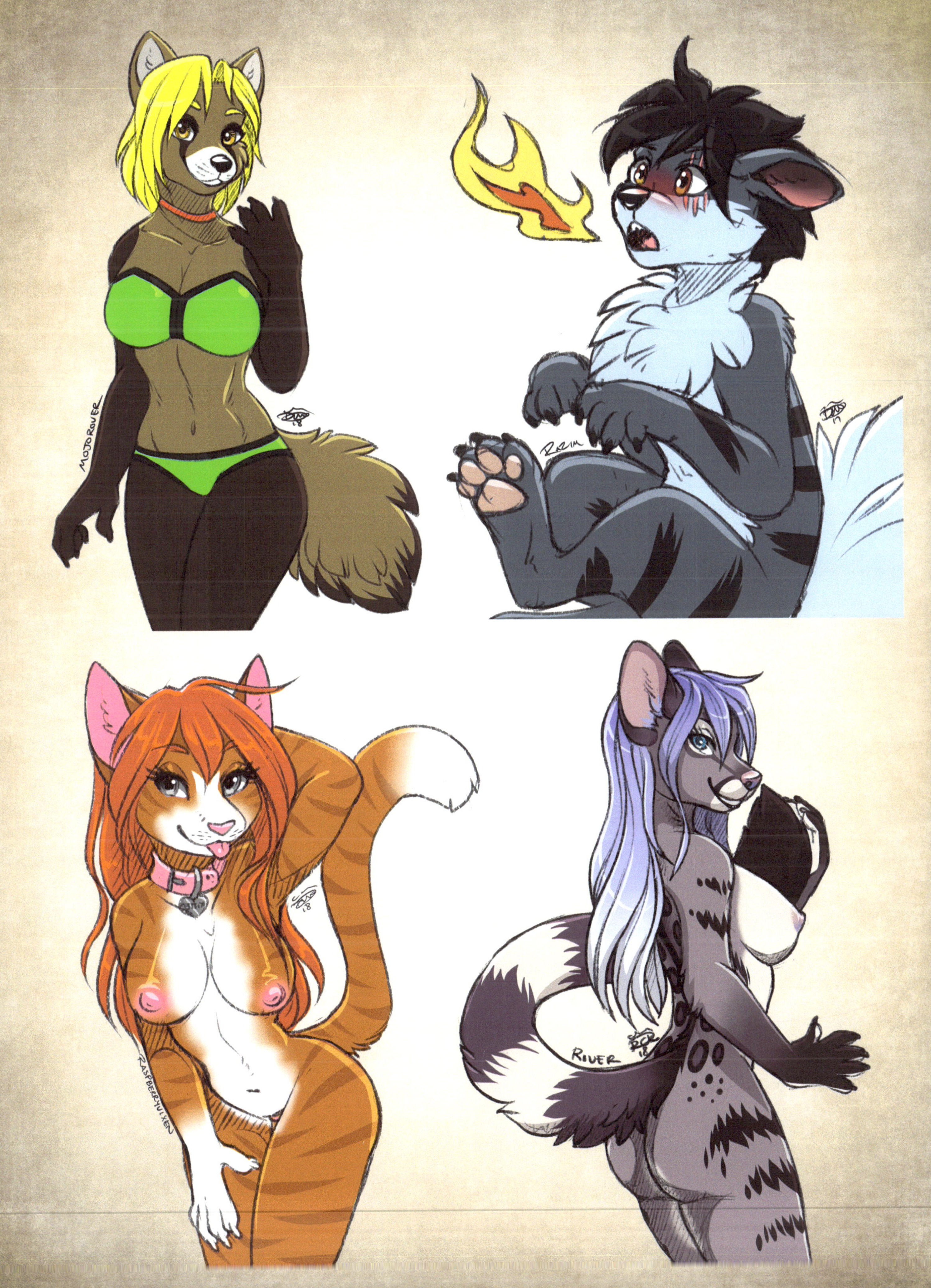

MOJOROVER
RAZIM
RASPBERRYVIXEN
RIVER

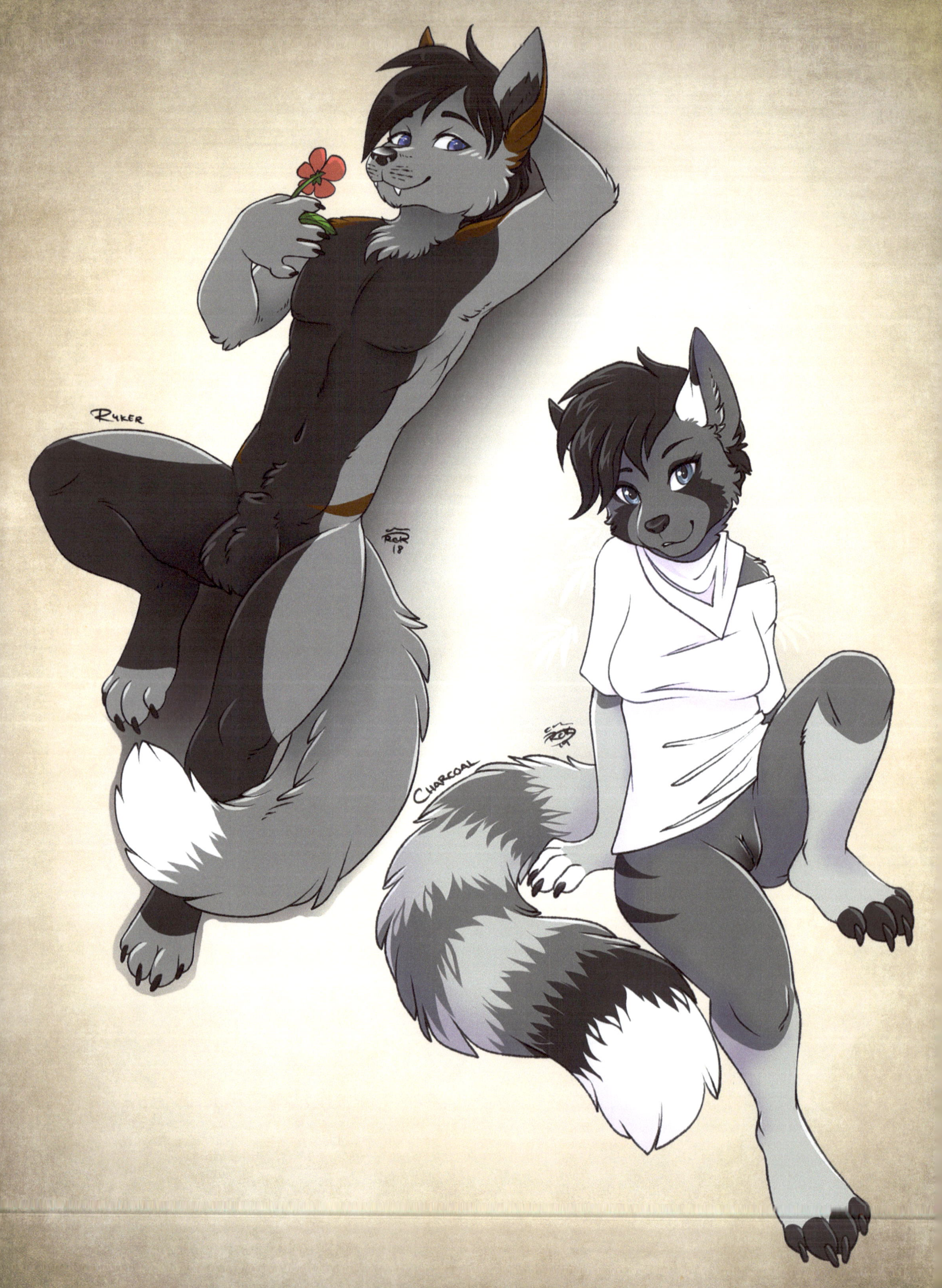
Ryker
Charcoal

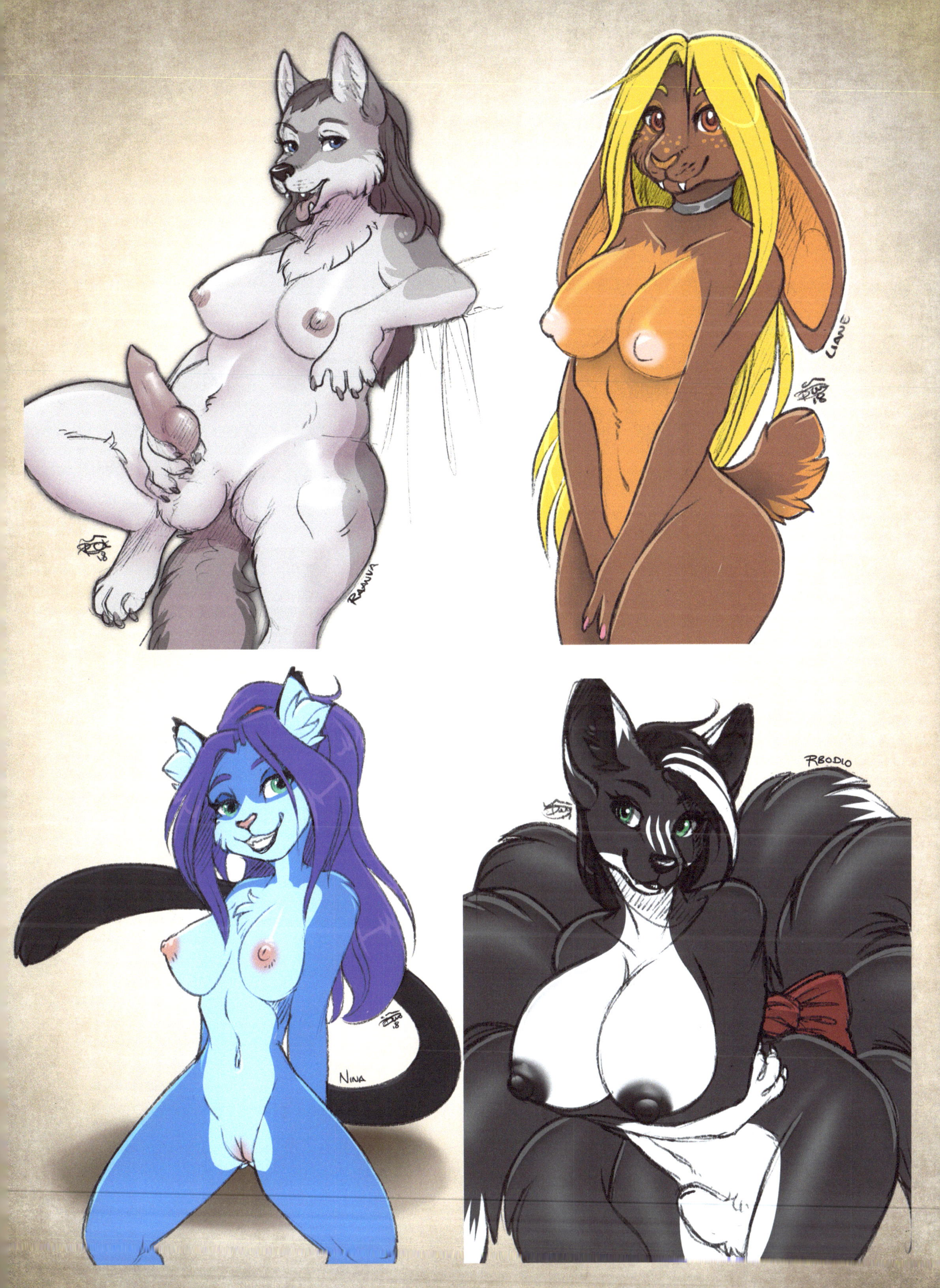

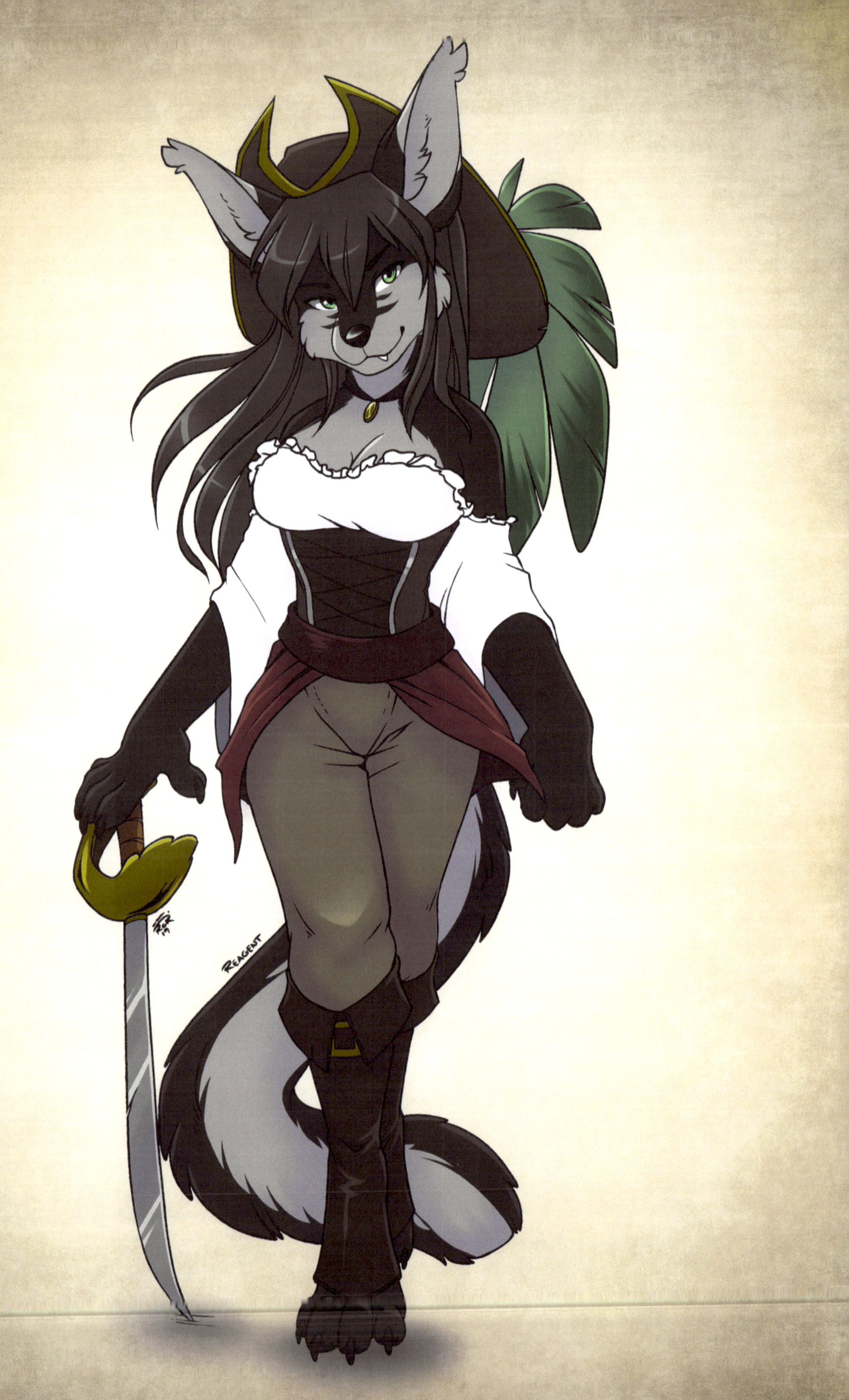
REAGENT

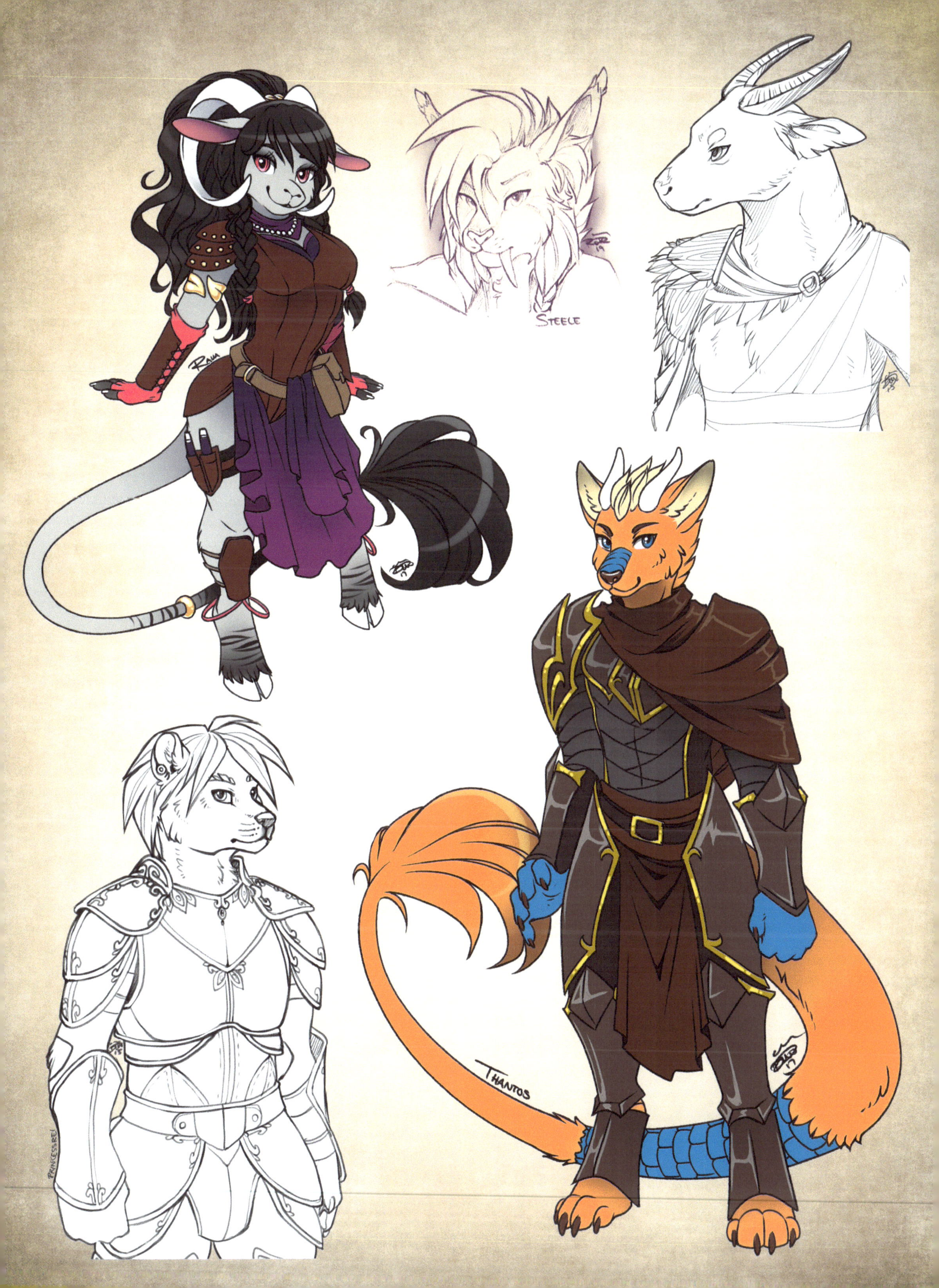
Raum
Steele
Thantos
PRINCESSREI

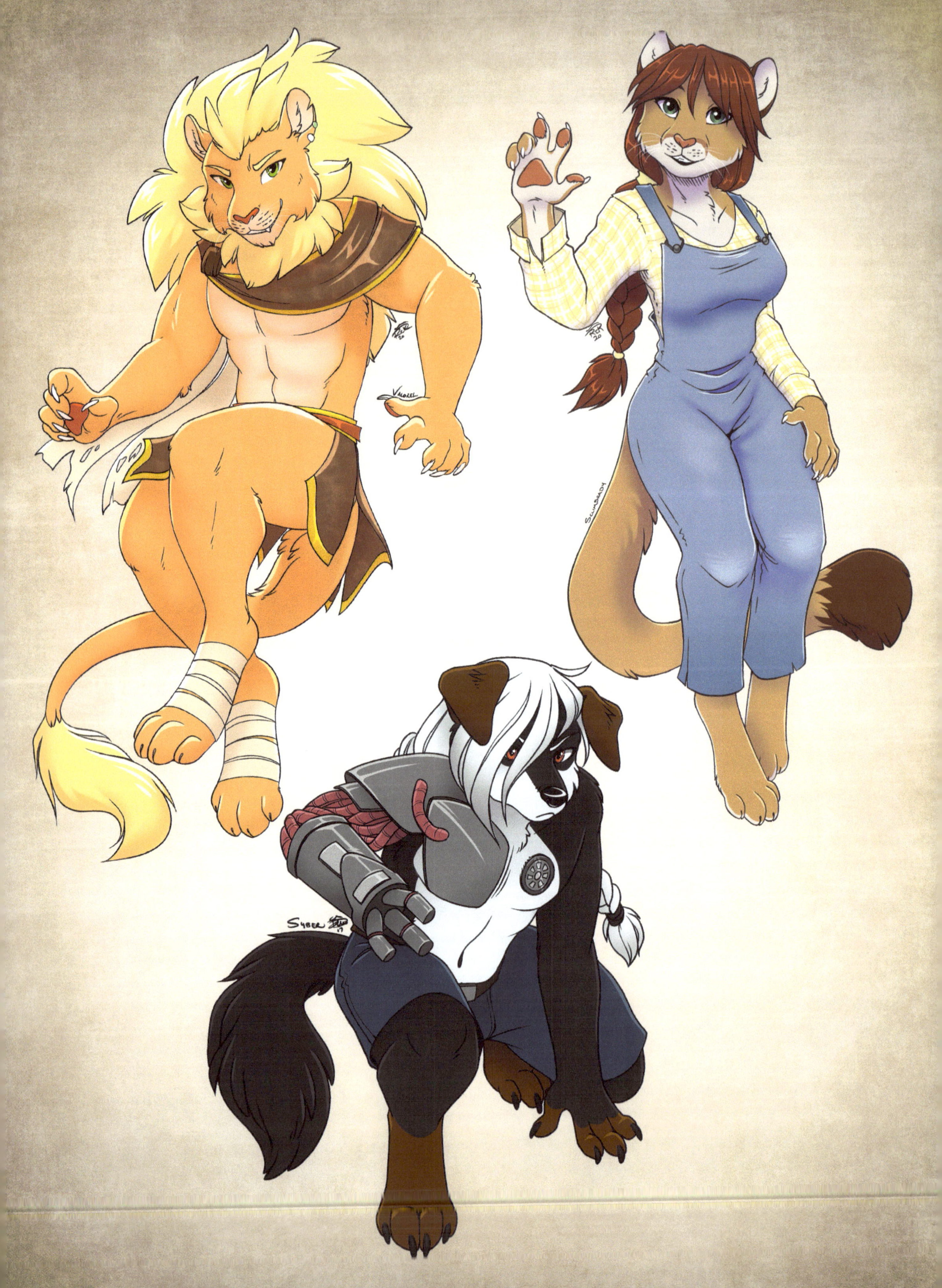
Valorel
Scumbady
Syber

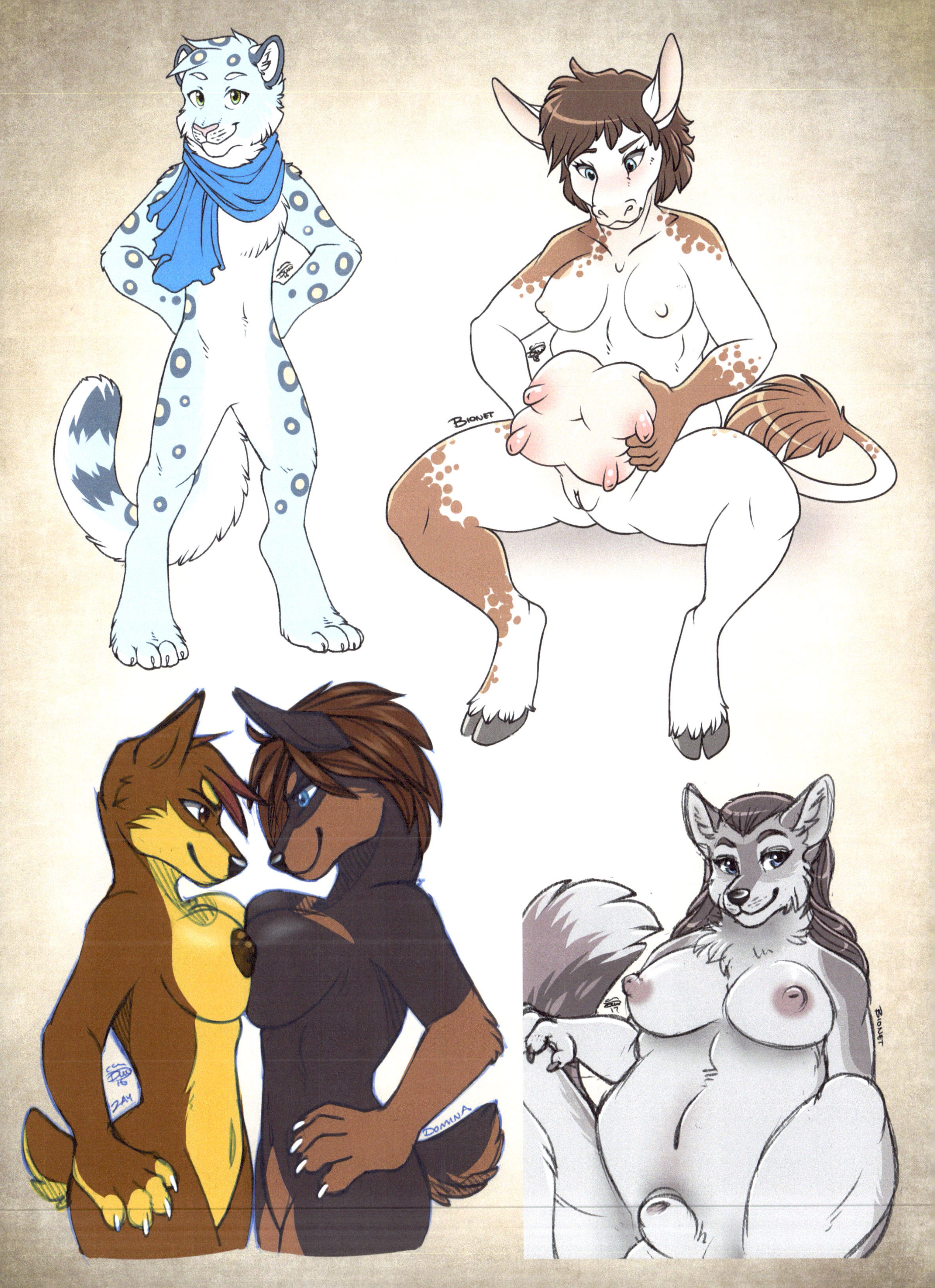
BIONET
ZAY
DOMINA
BIONET

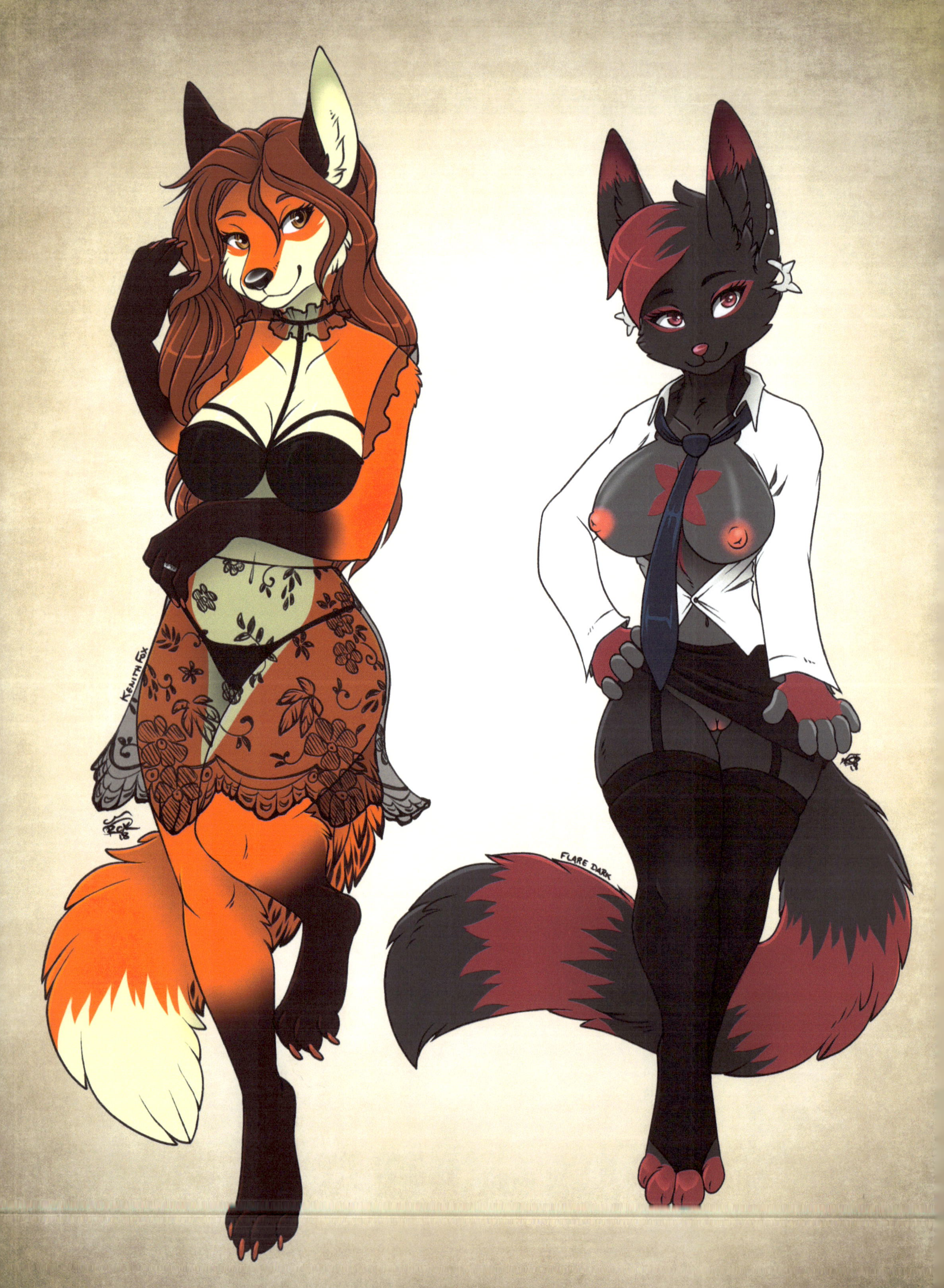
KENITH FOX
FLARE DARK

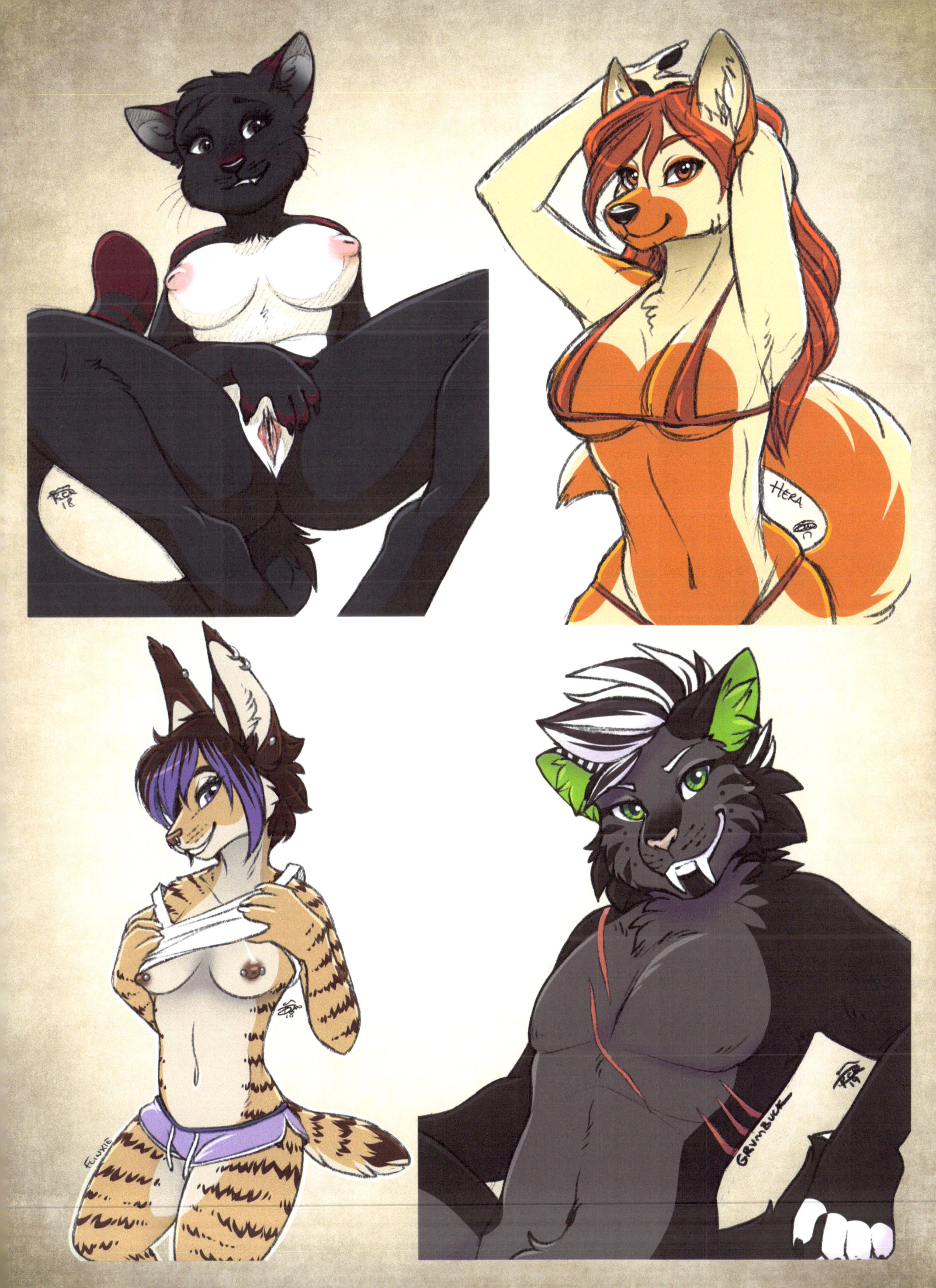
HERA
FLINXIE
GRUMBUCK

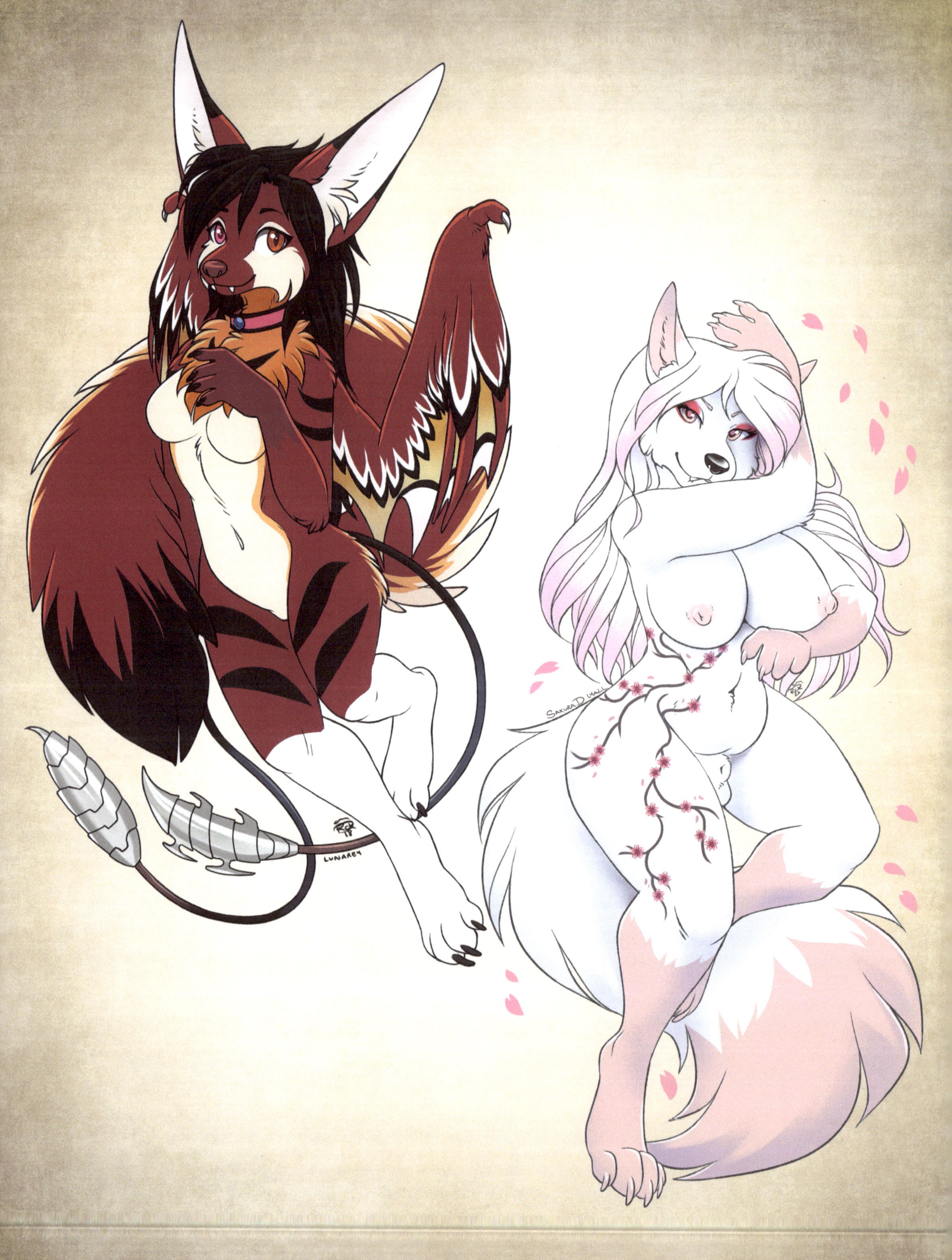
LUNAREY
SAKURA D LYALL

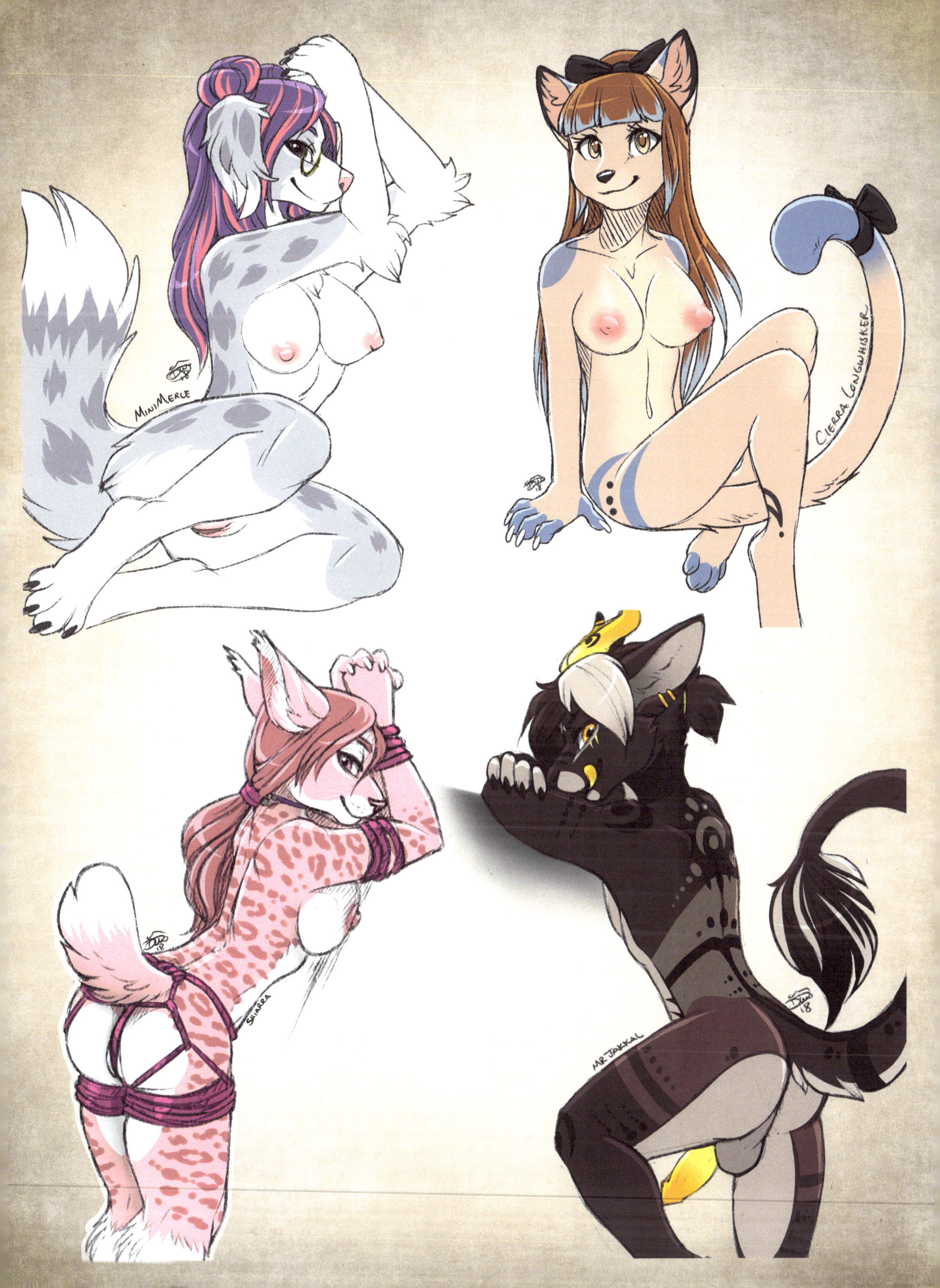
MiniMerle
Cierra Longwhisker
Shiarra
Mr.Jakkal

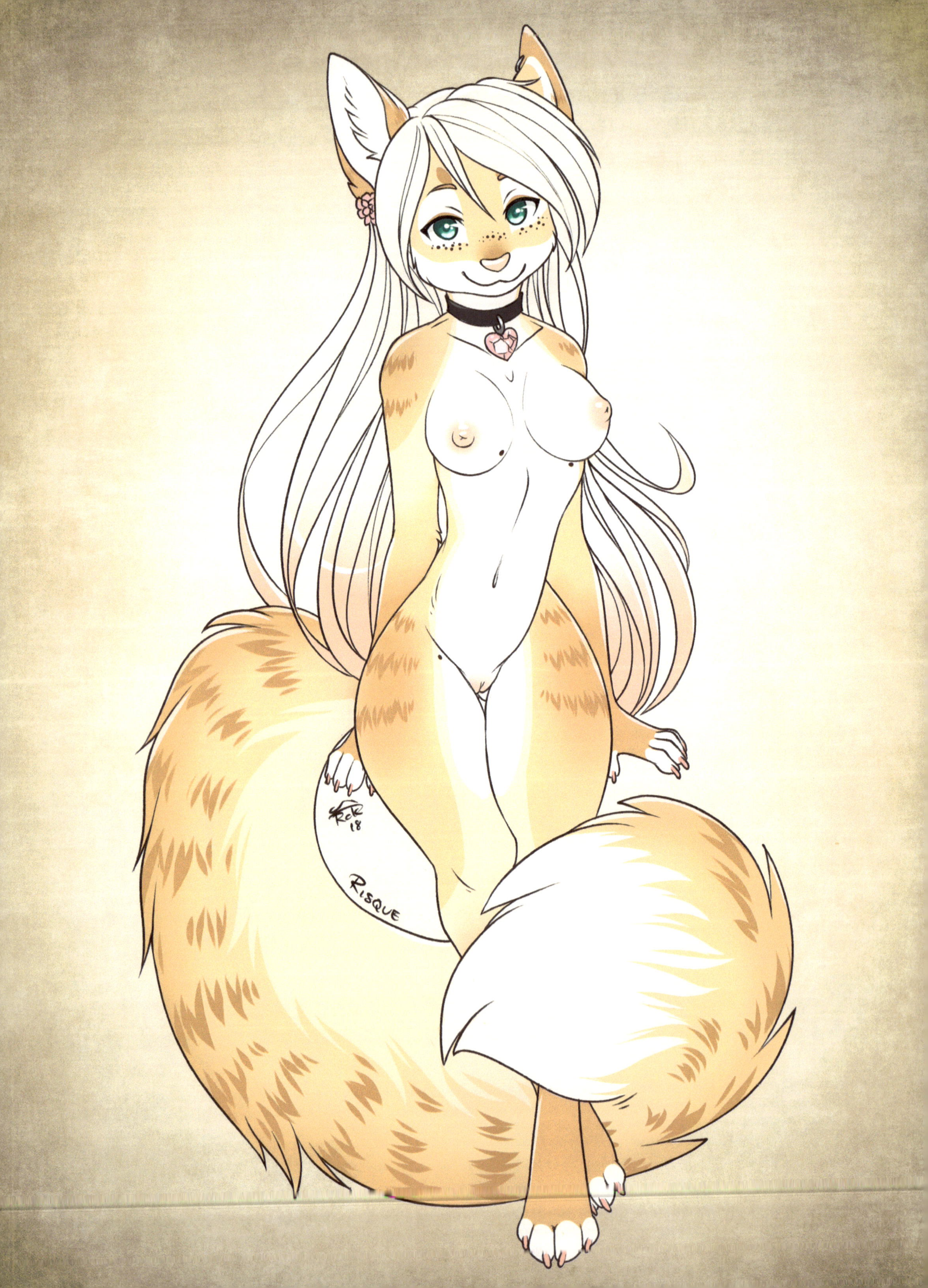
RcK
18
Risque

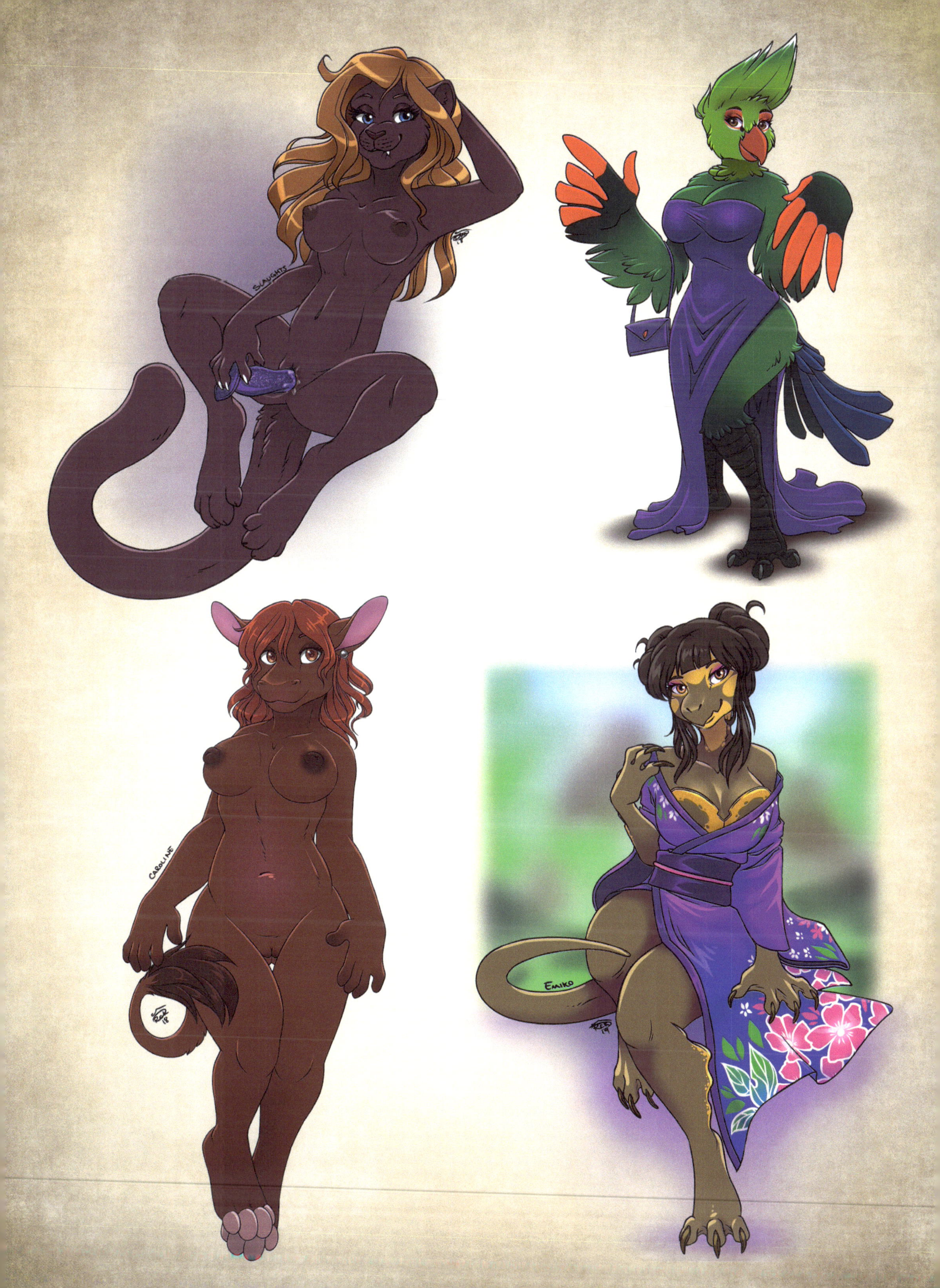
SLAUGHTS
CAROLINE
EMIKO

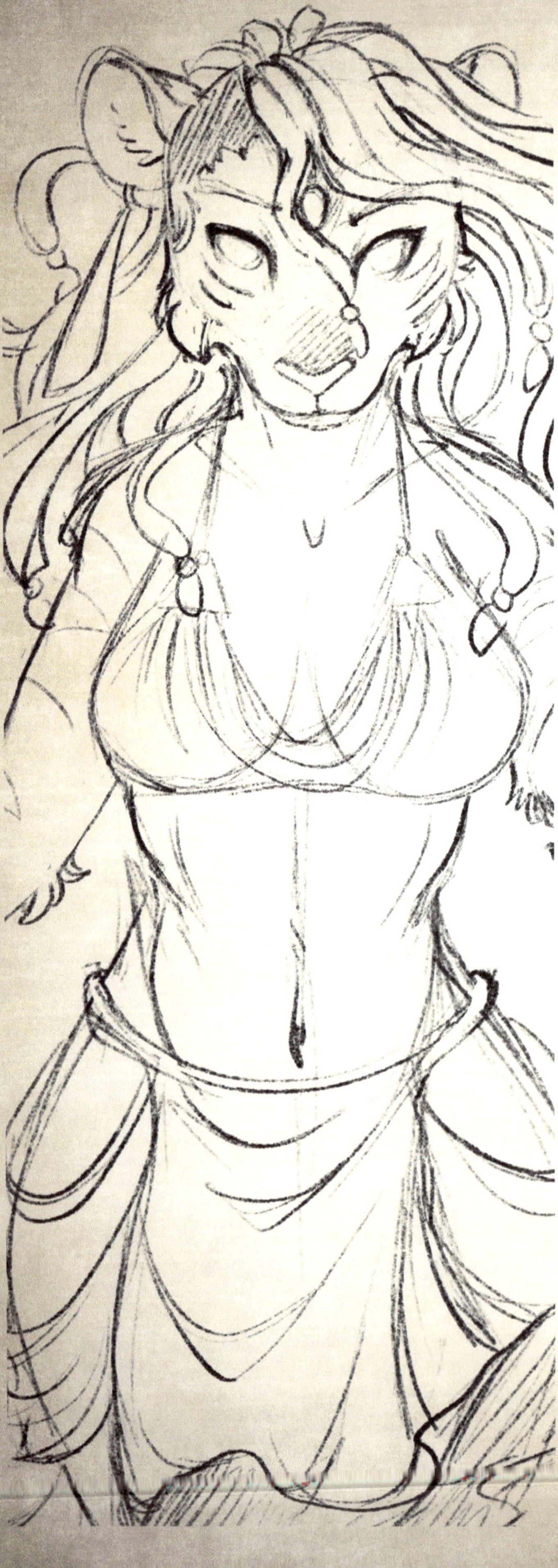

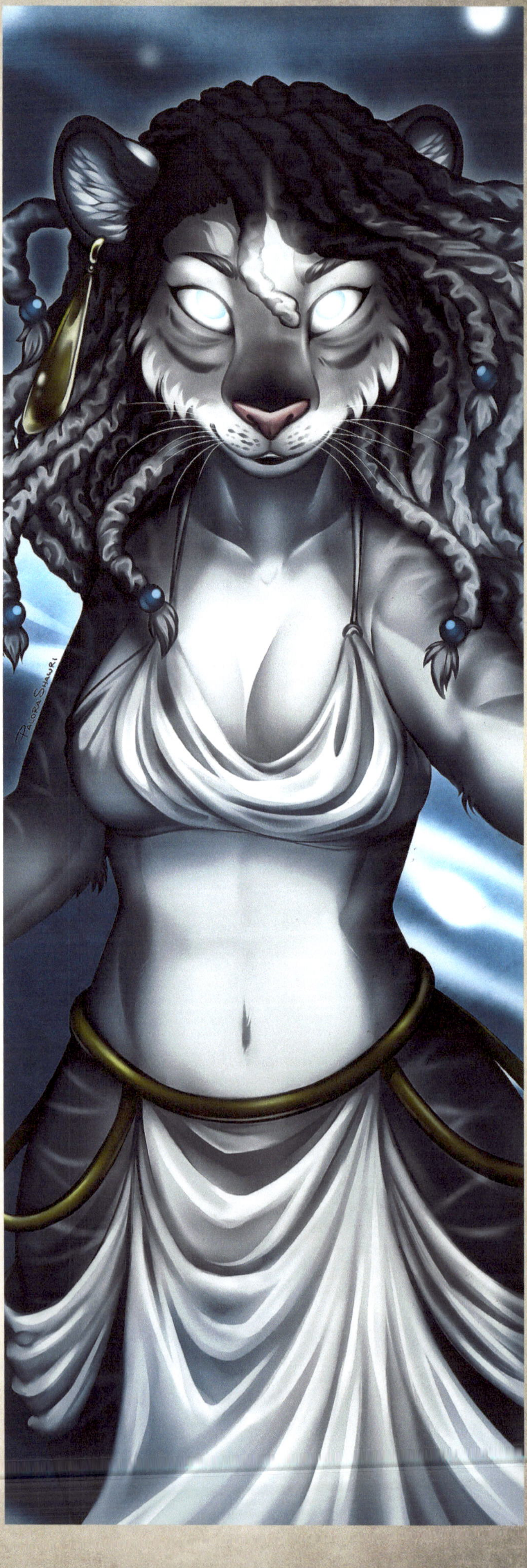

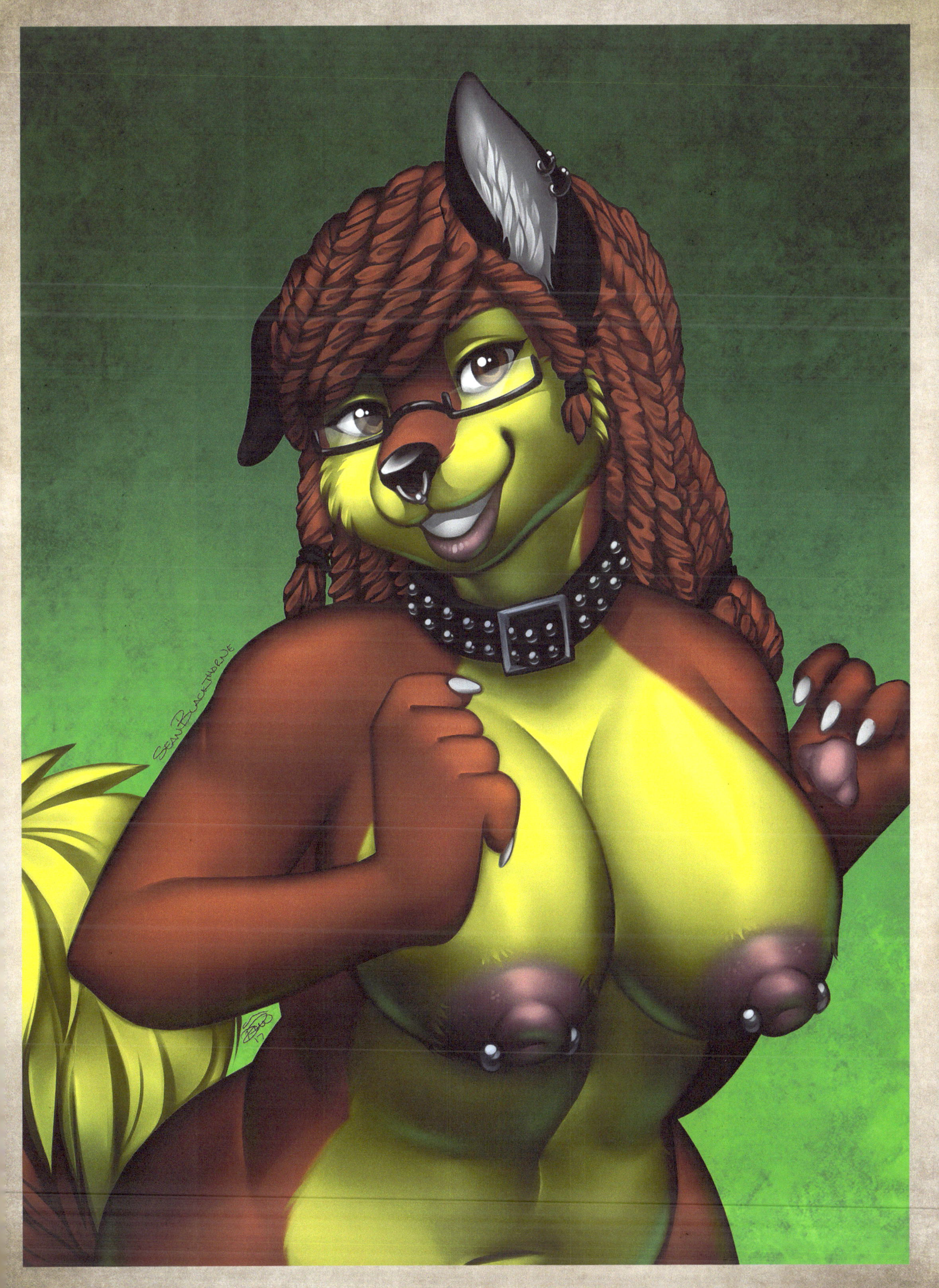

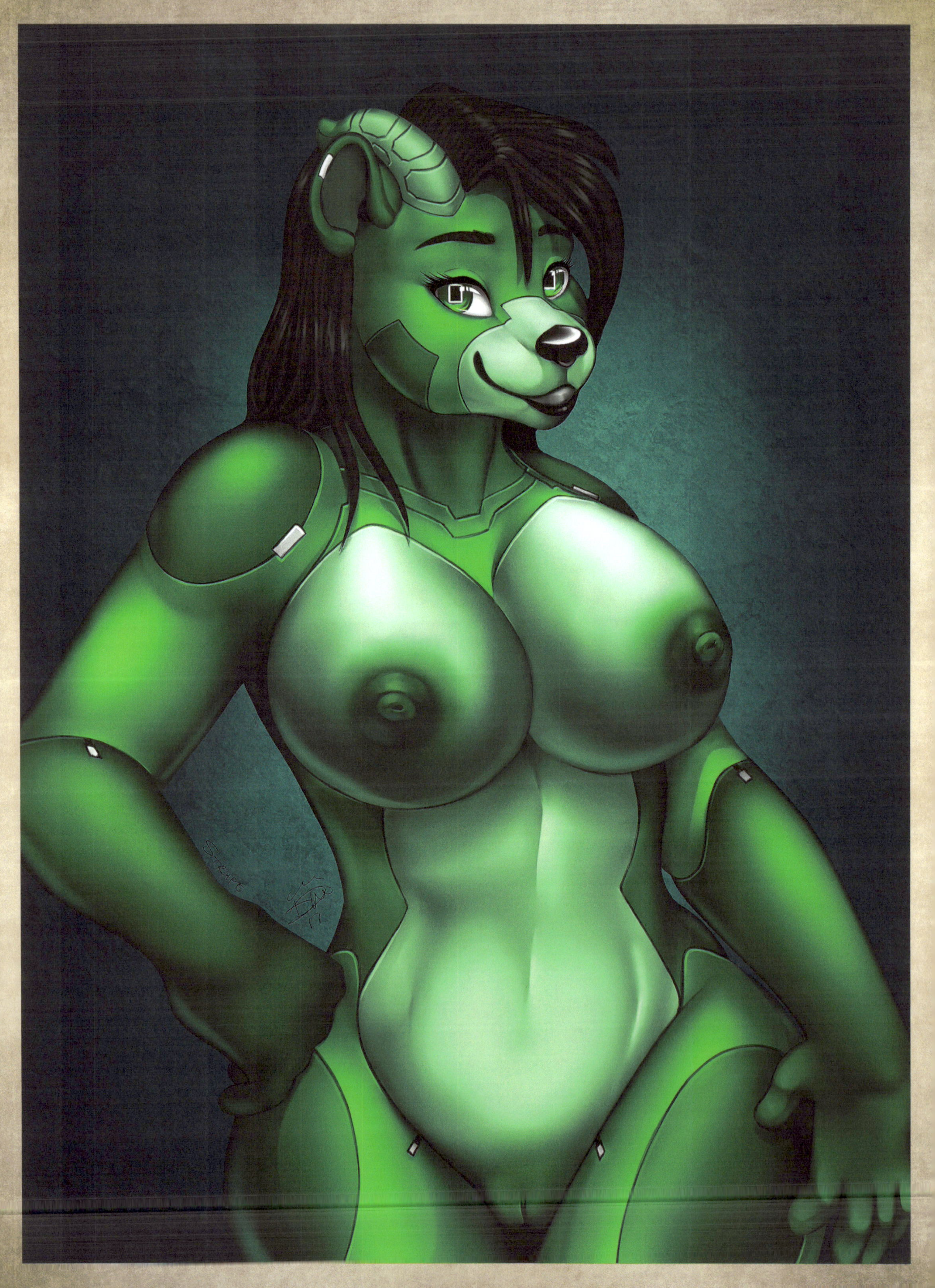

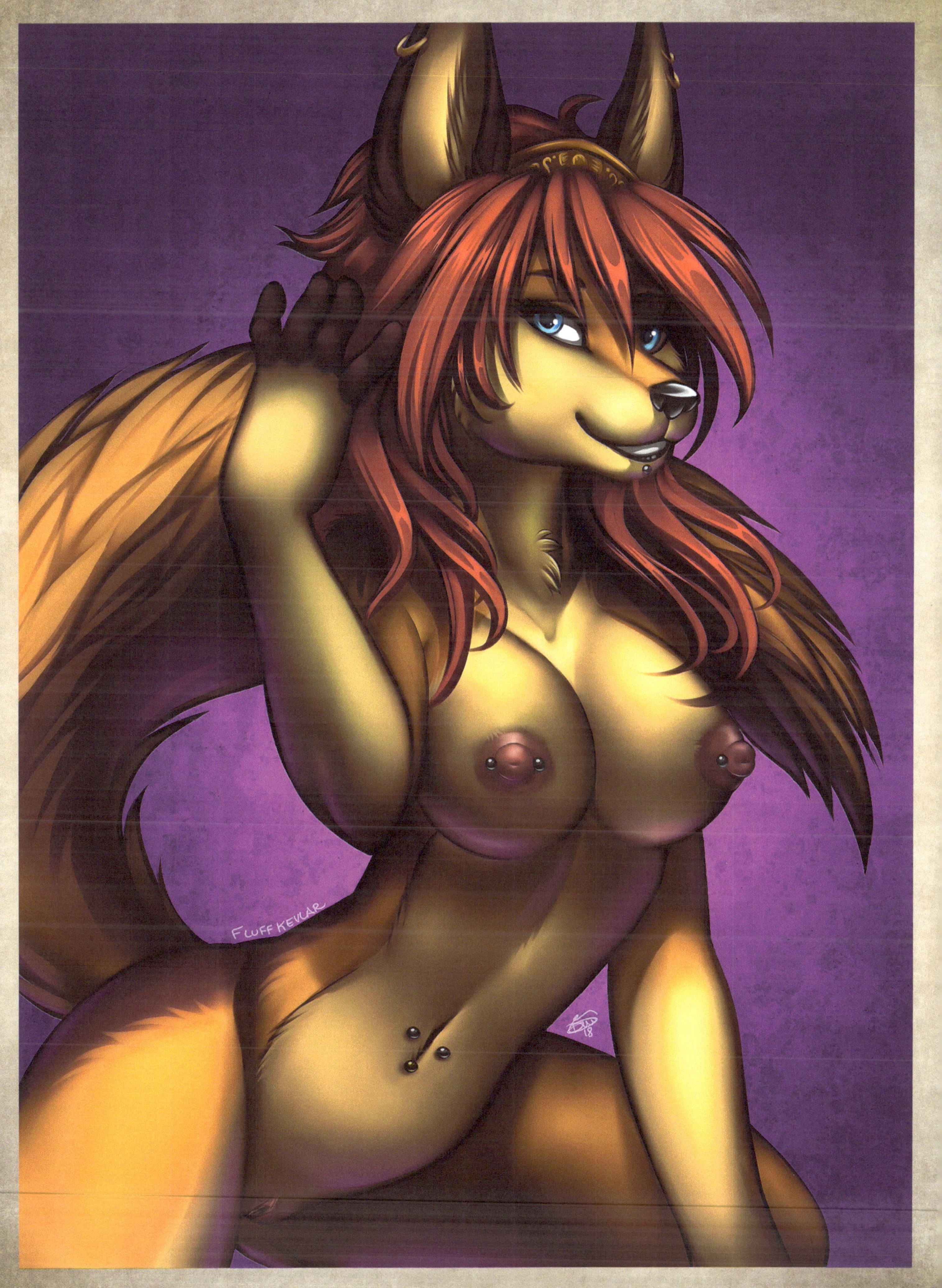
FLUFFKEVLAR

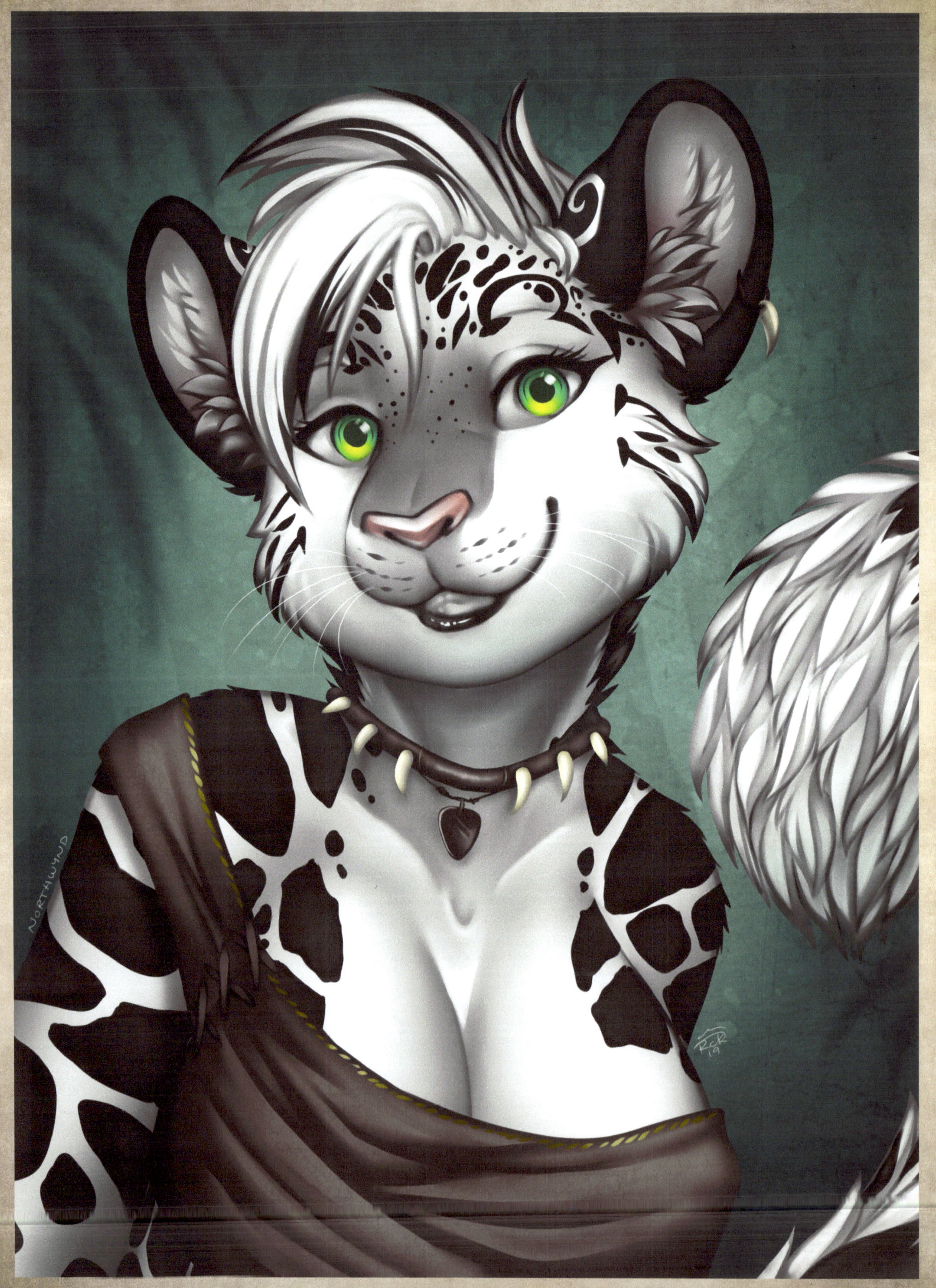
NORTHWYND
RCR
19

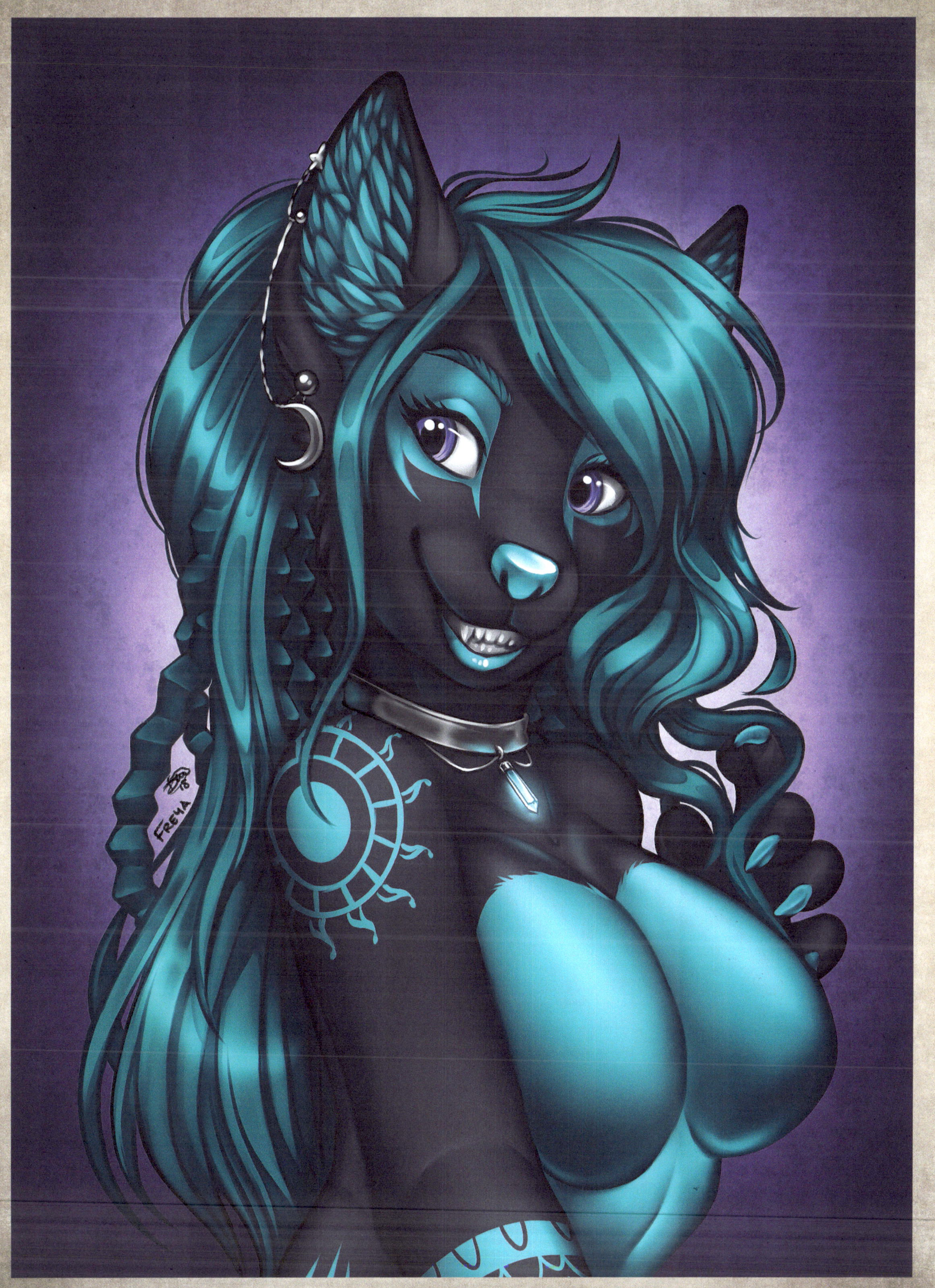
FREYA

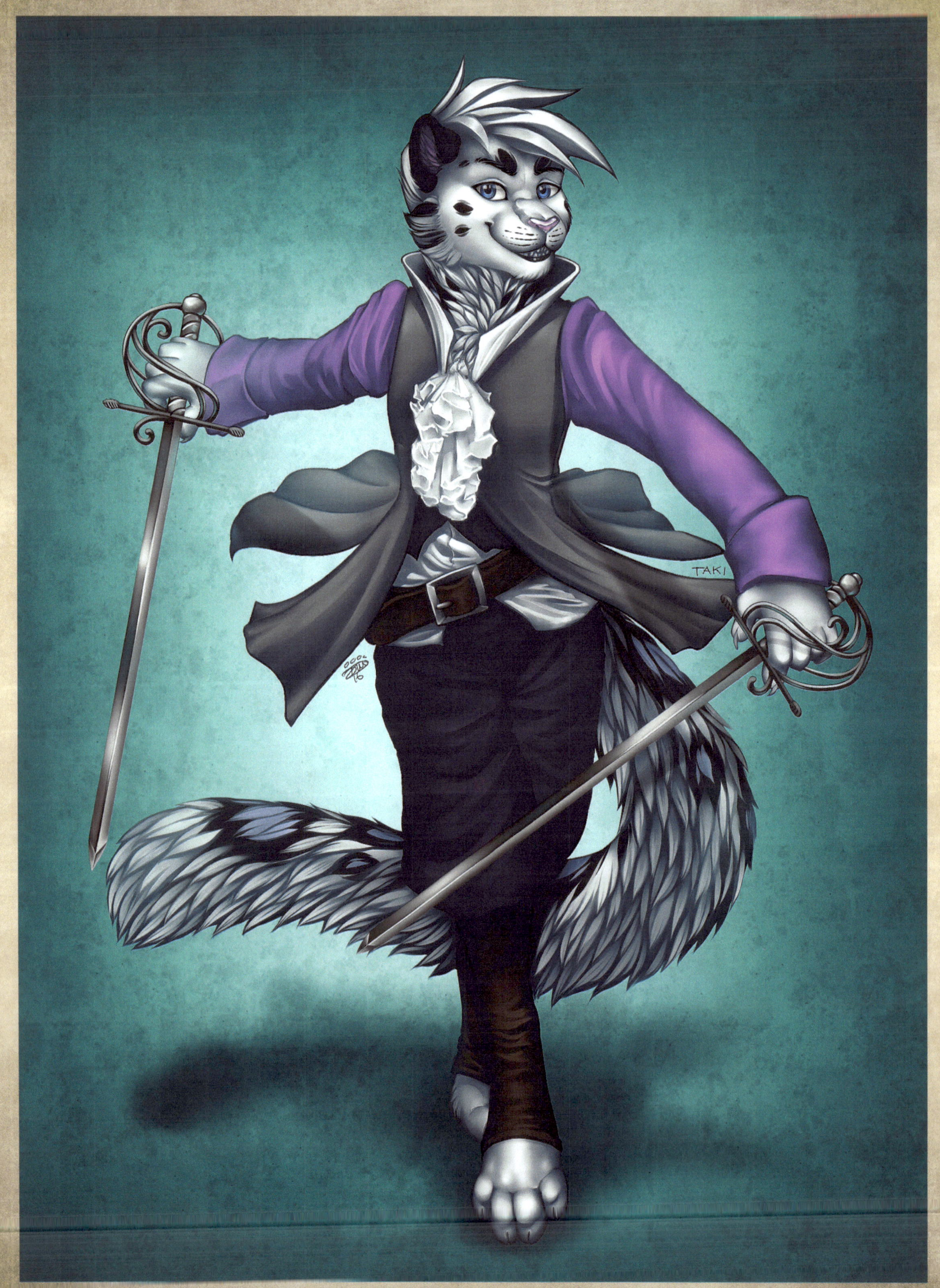
TAKI

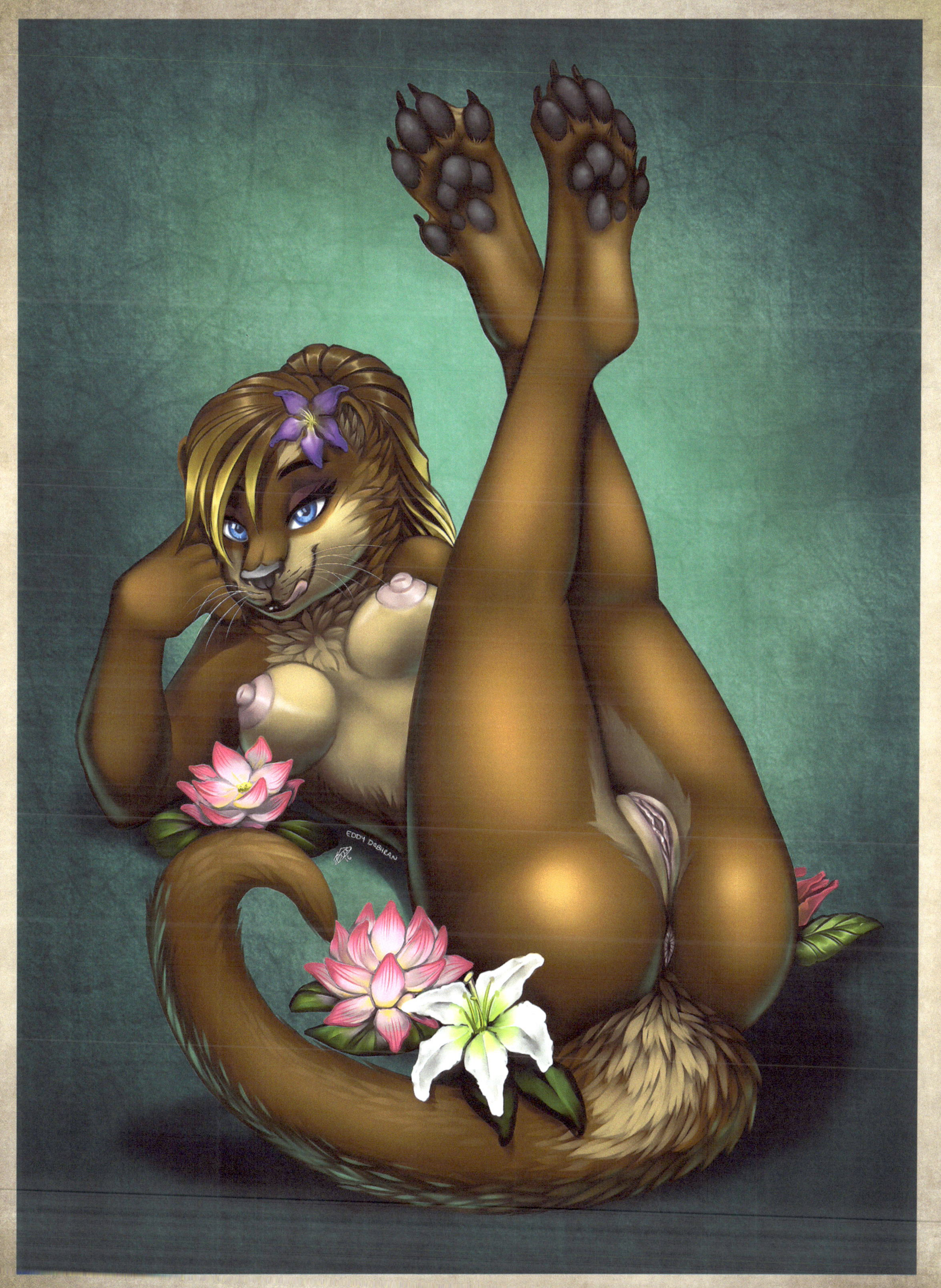
EDDY DOBHRAN

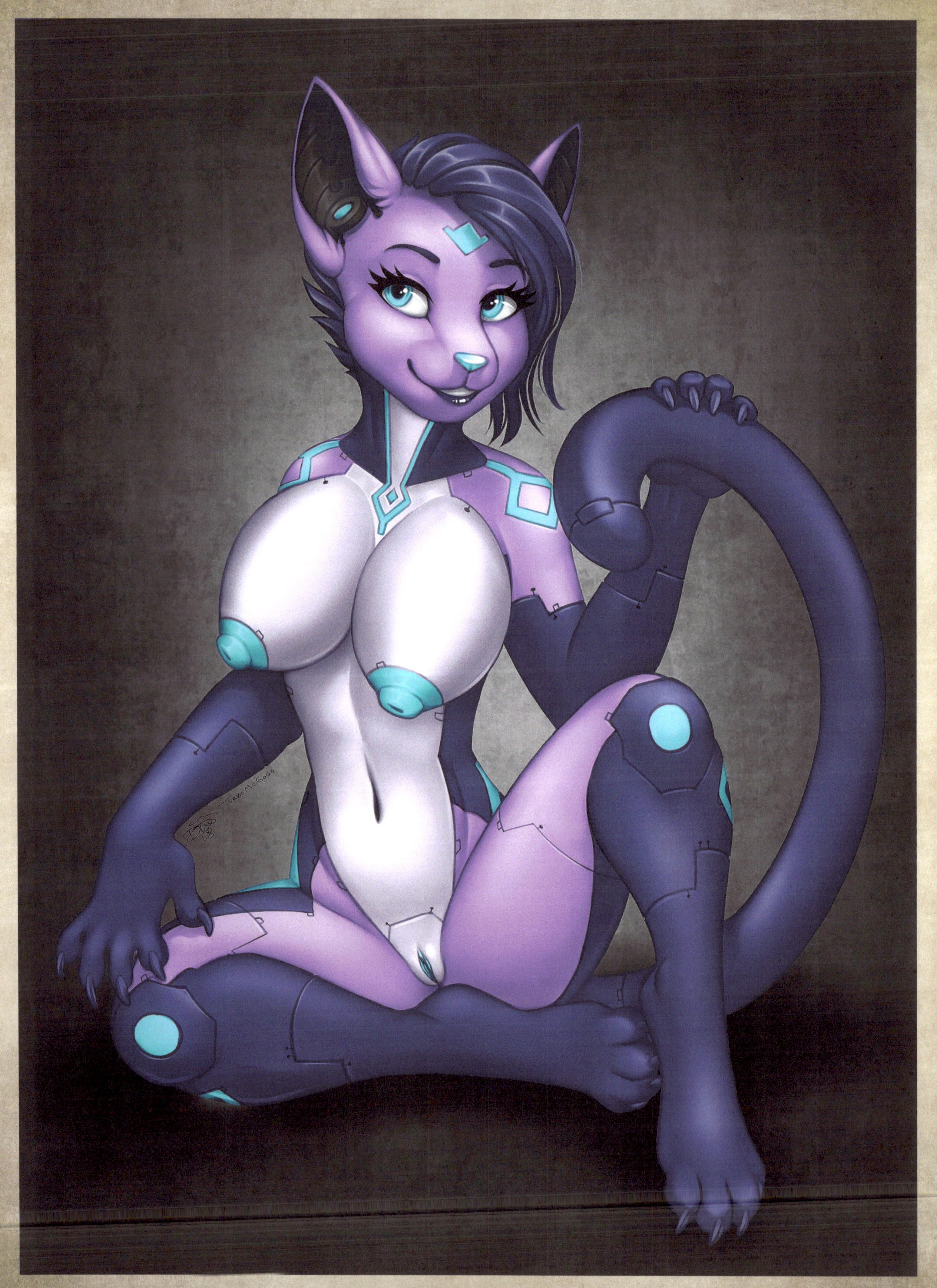
-TurboMcGogo

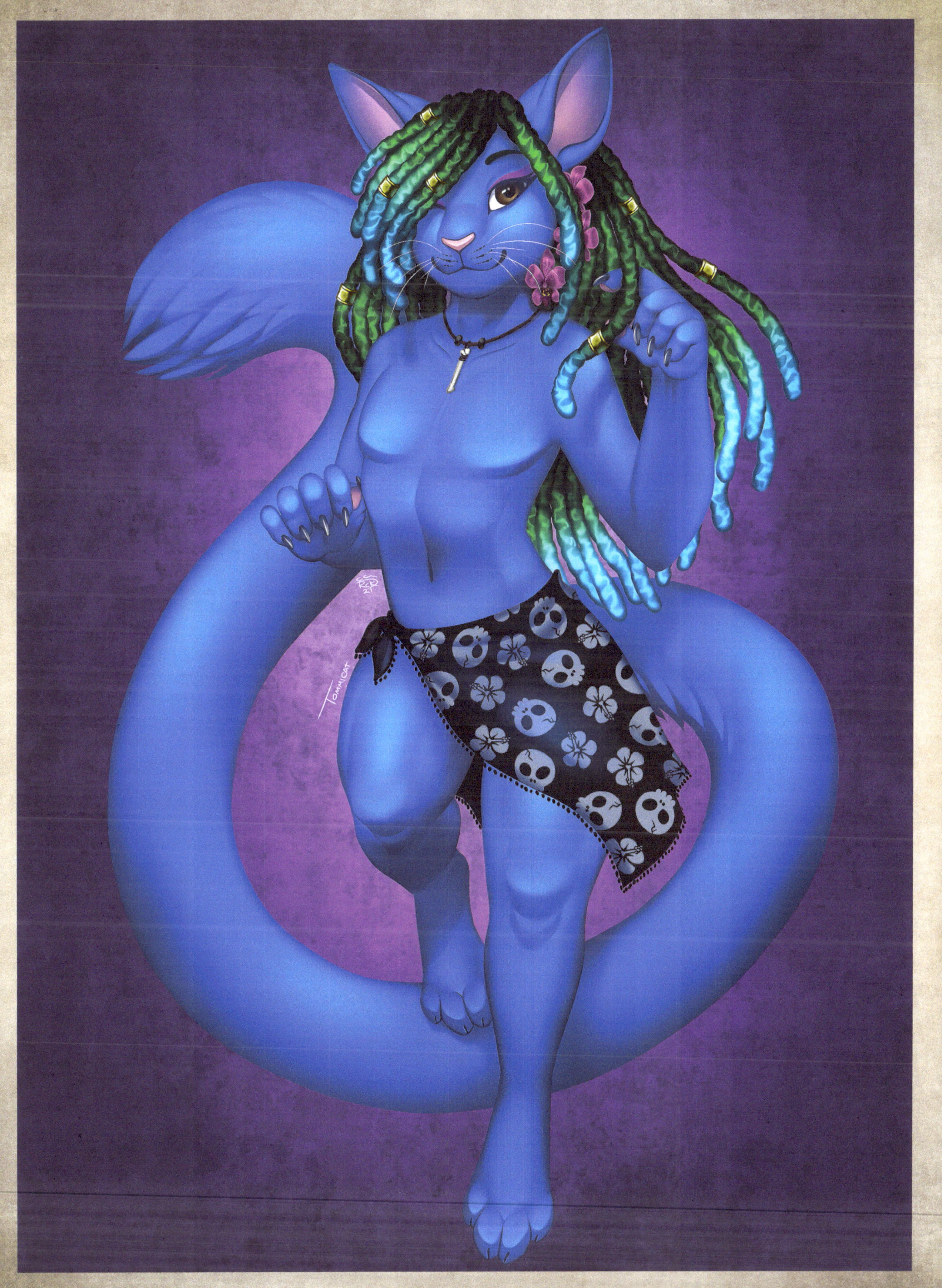
Tommicat

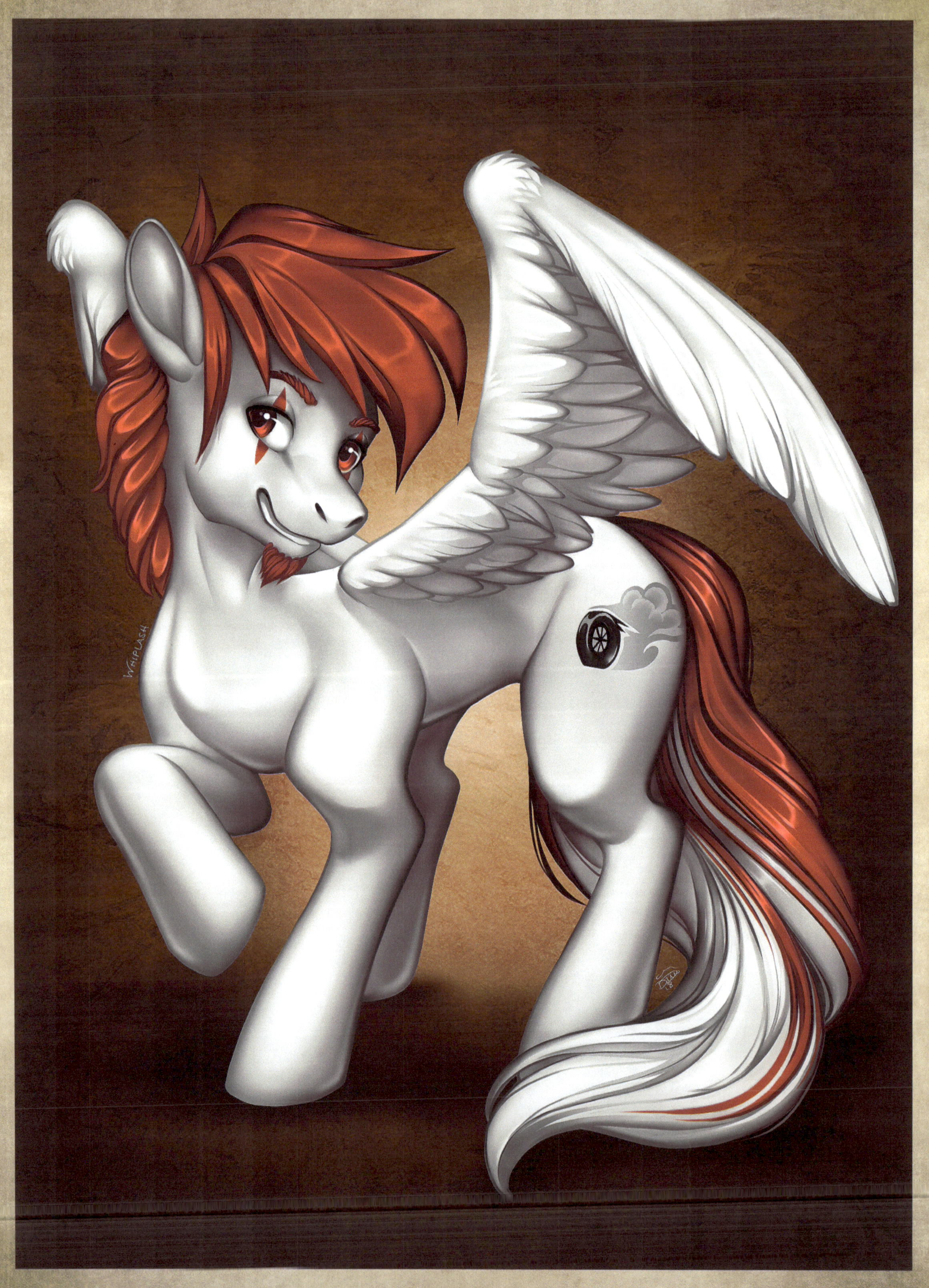
WHIPLASH

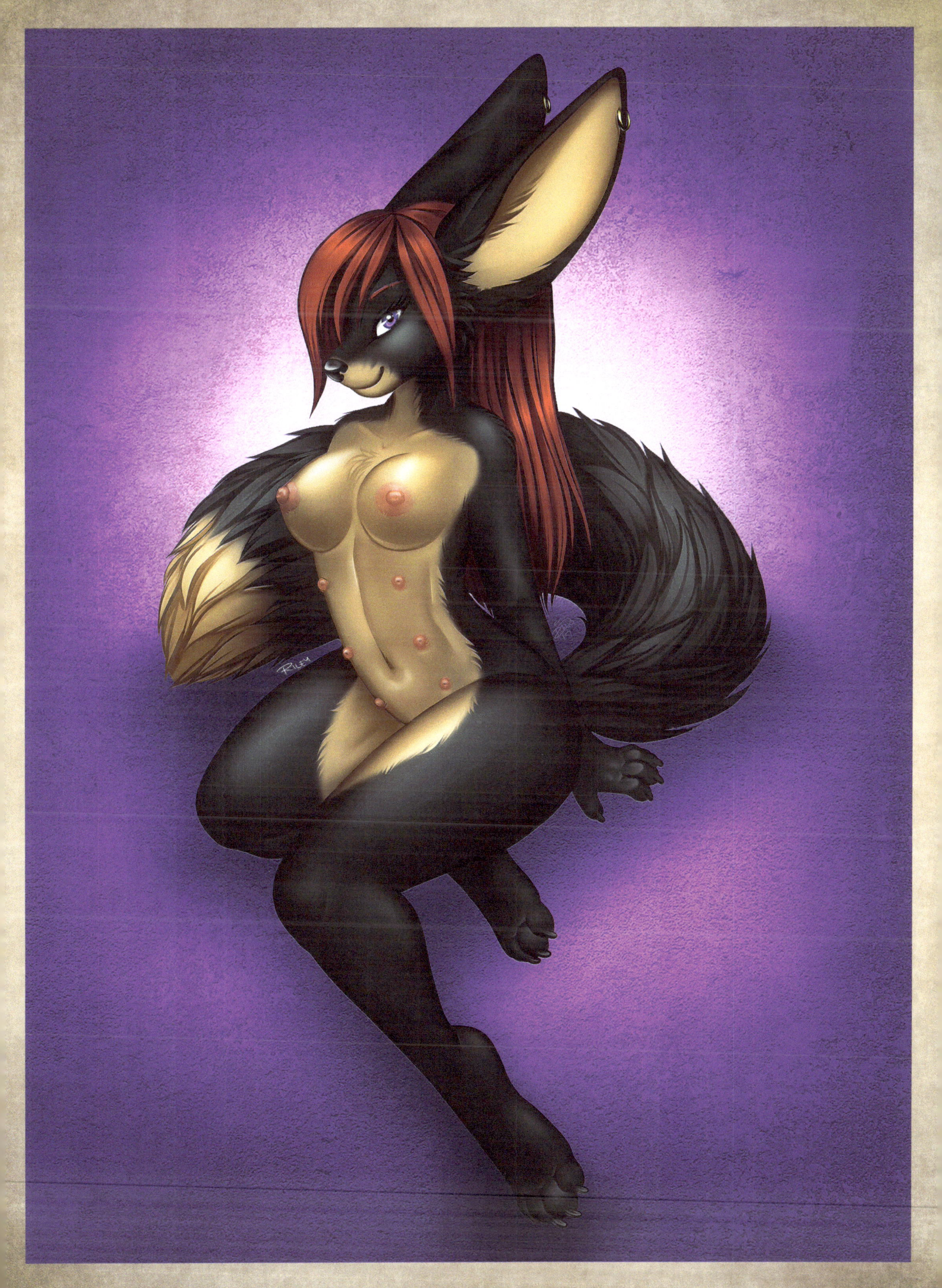

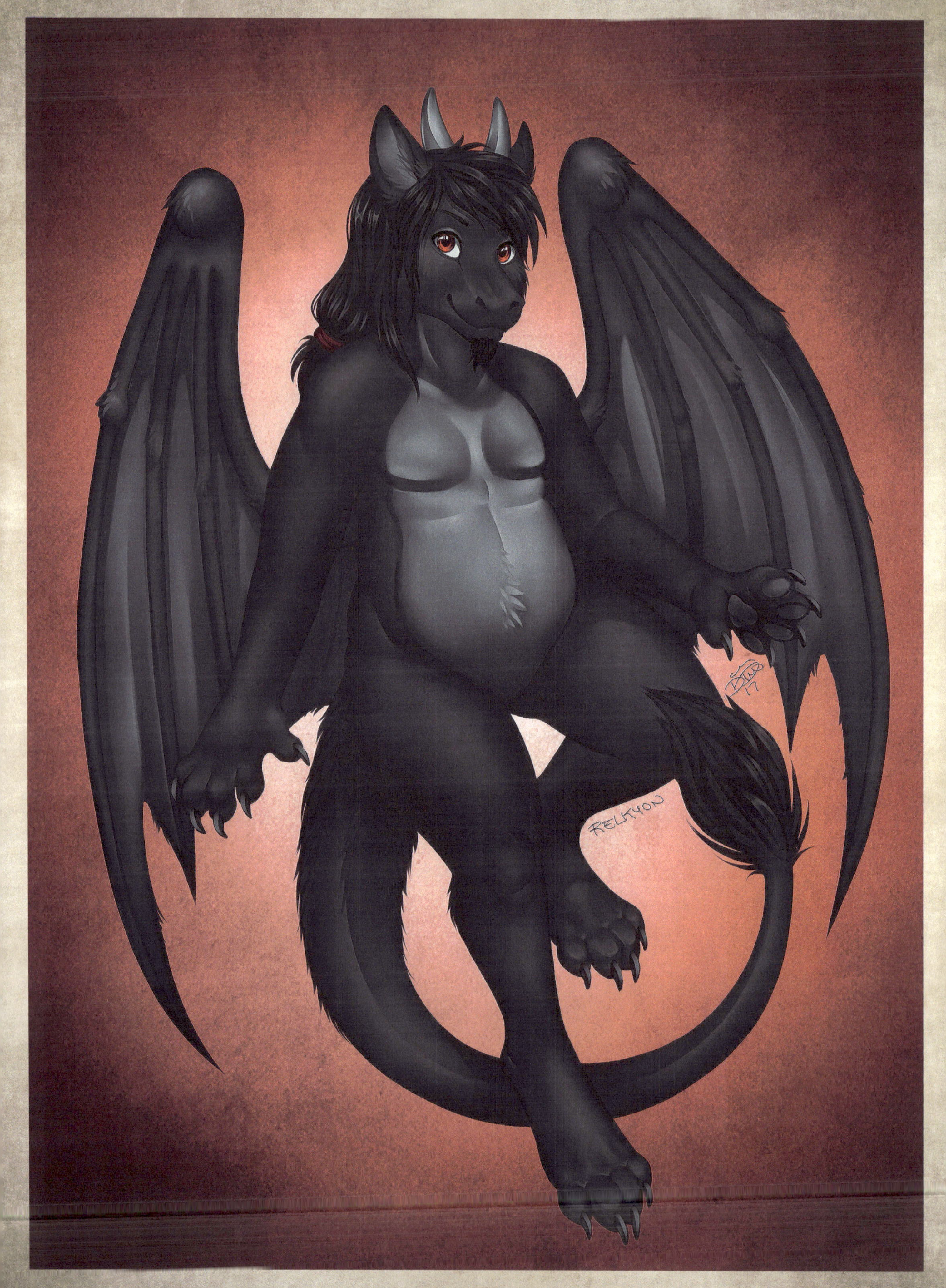
RELKYON

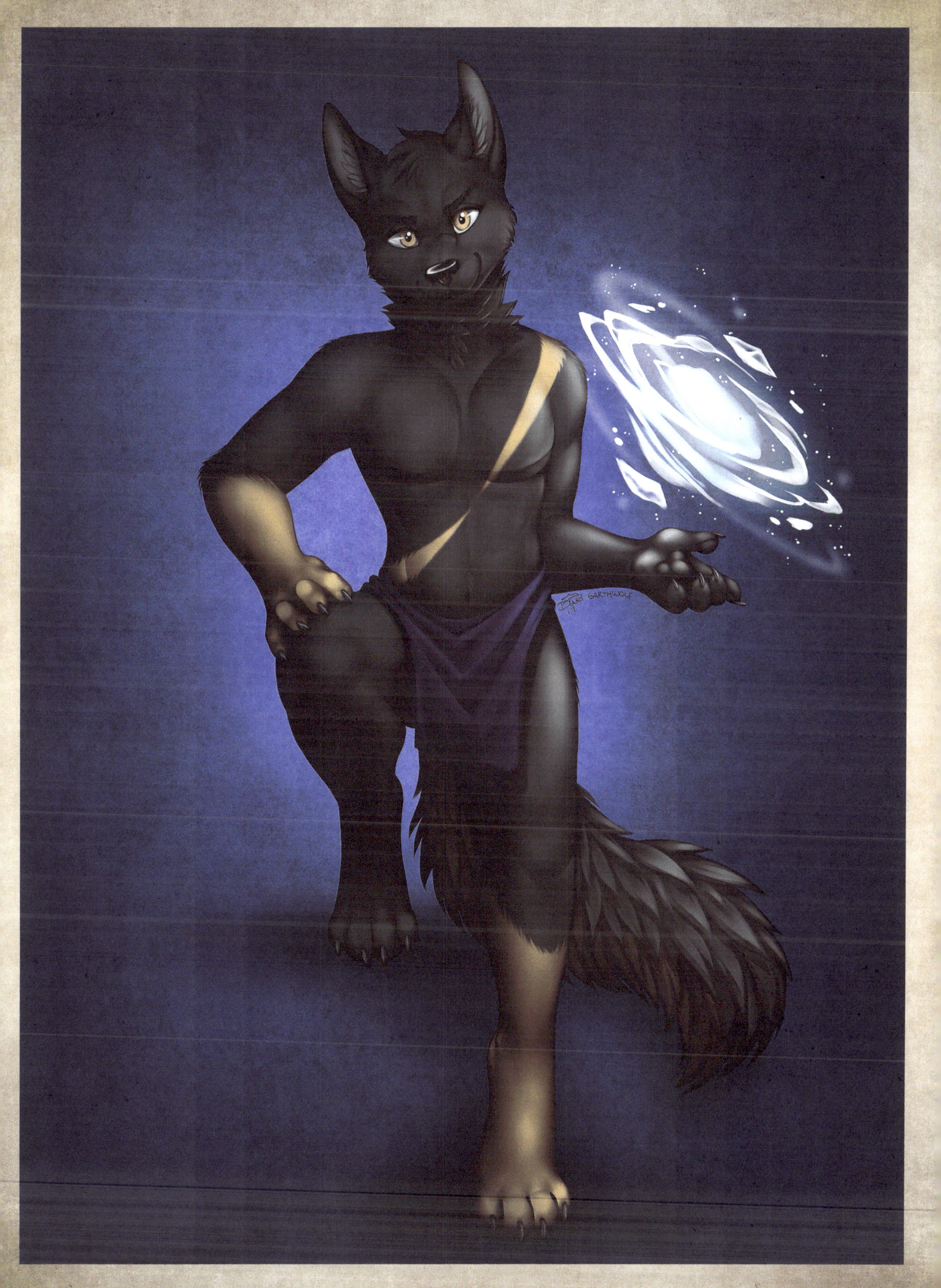
GARTHWOLF
17

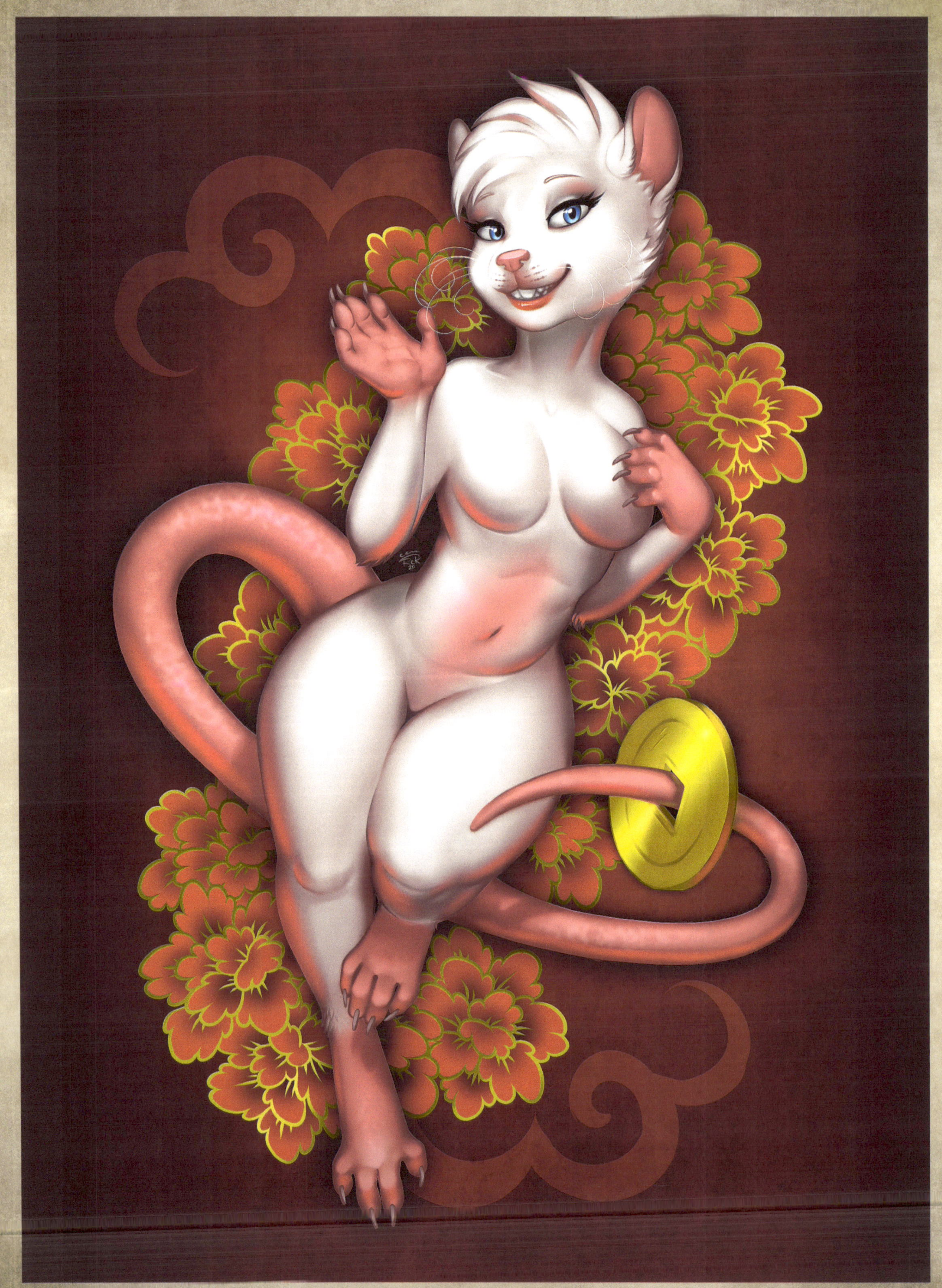

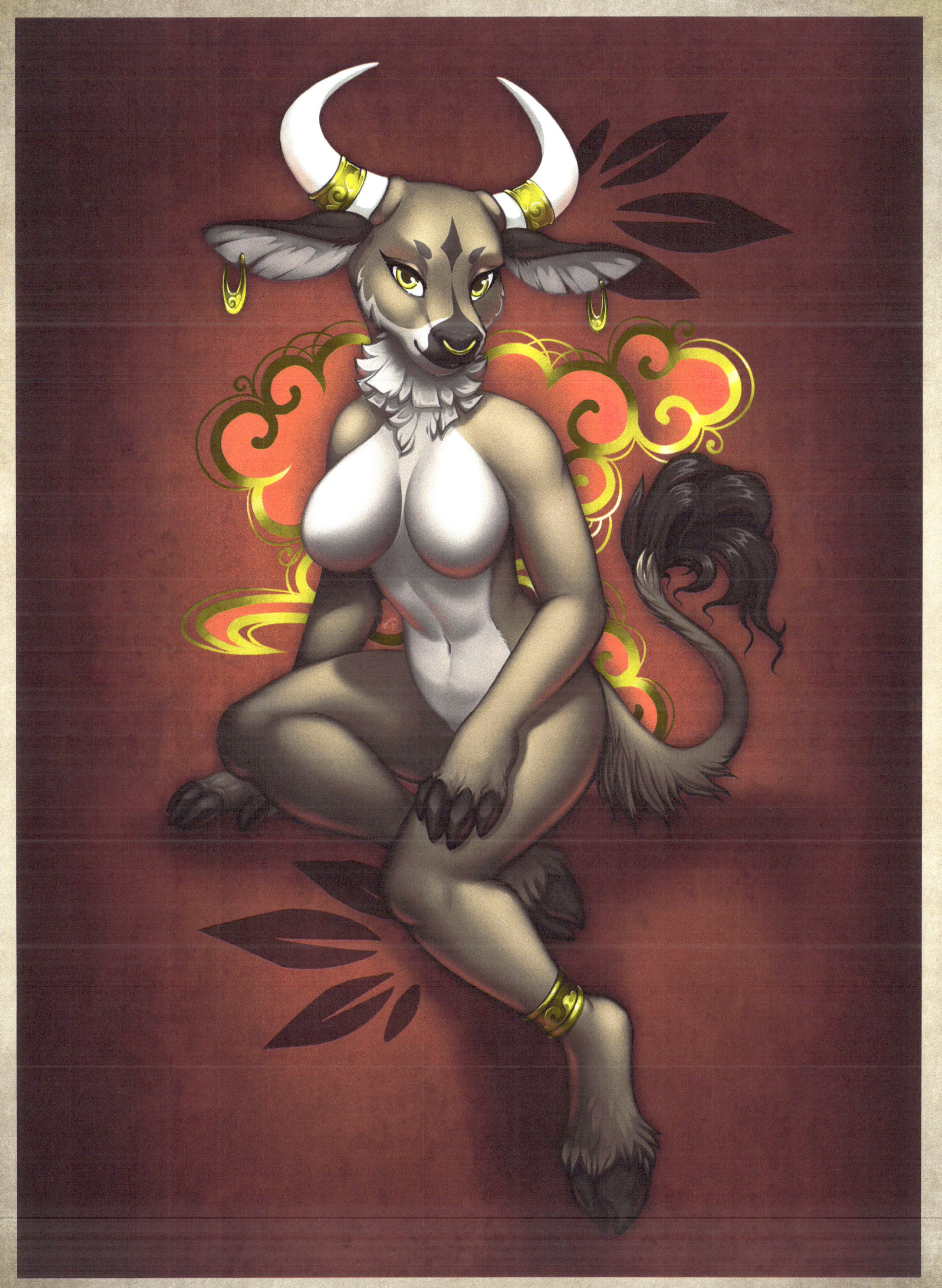

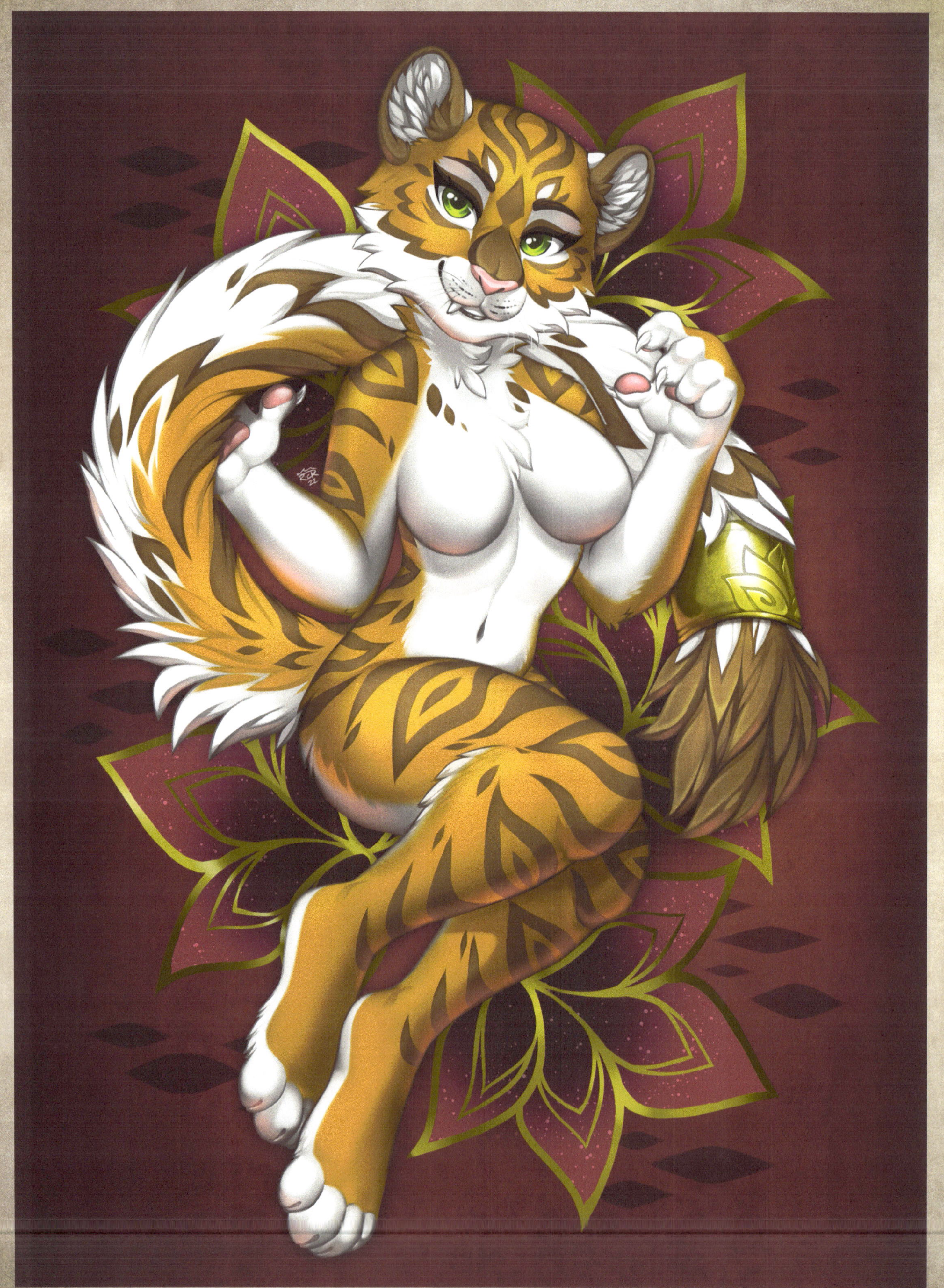

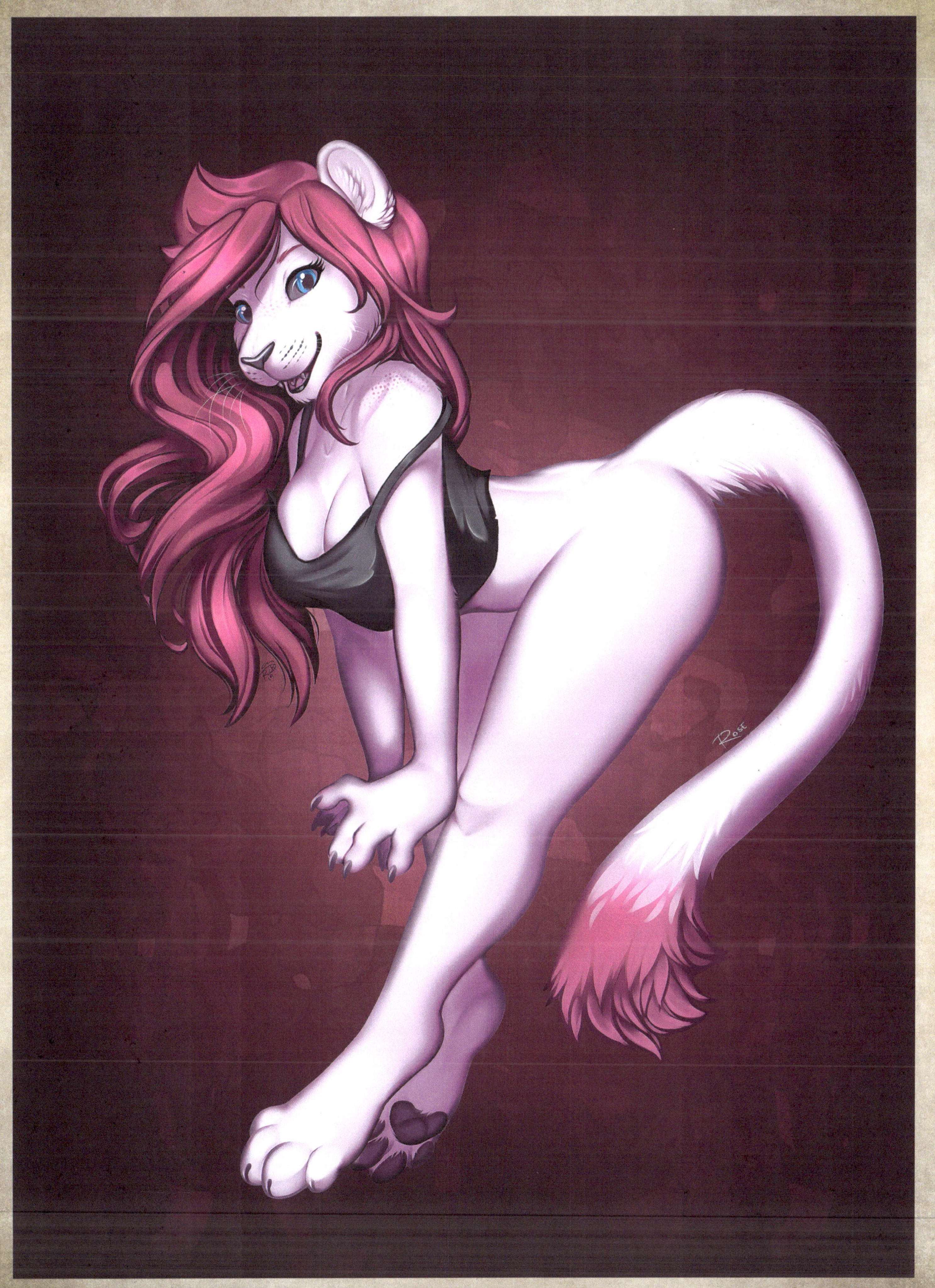
Rose

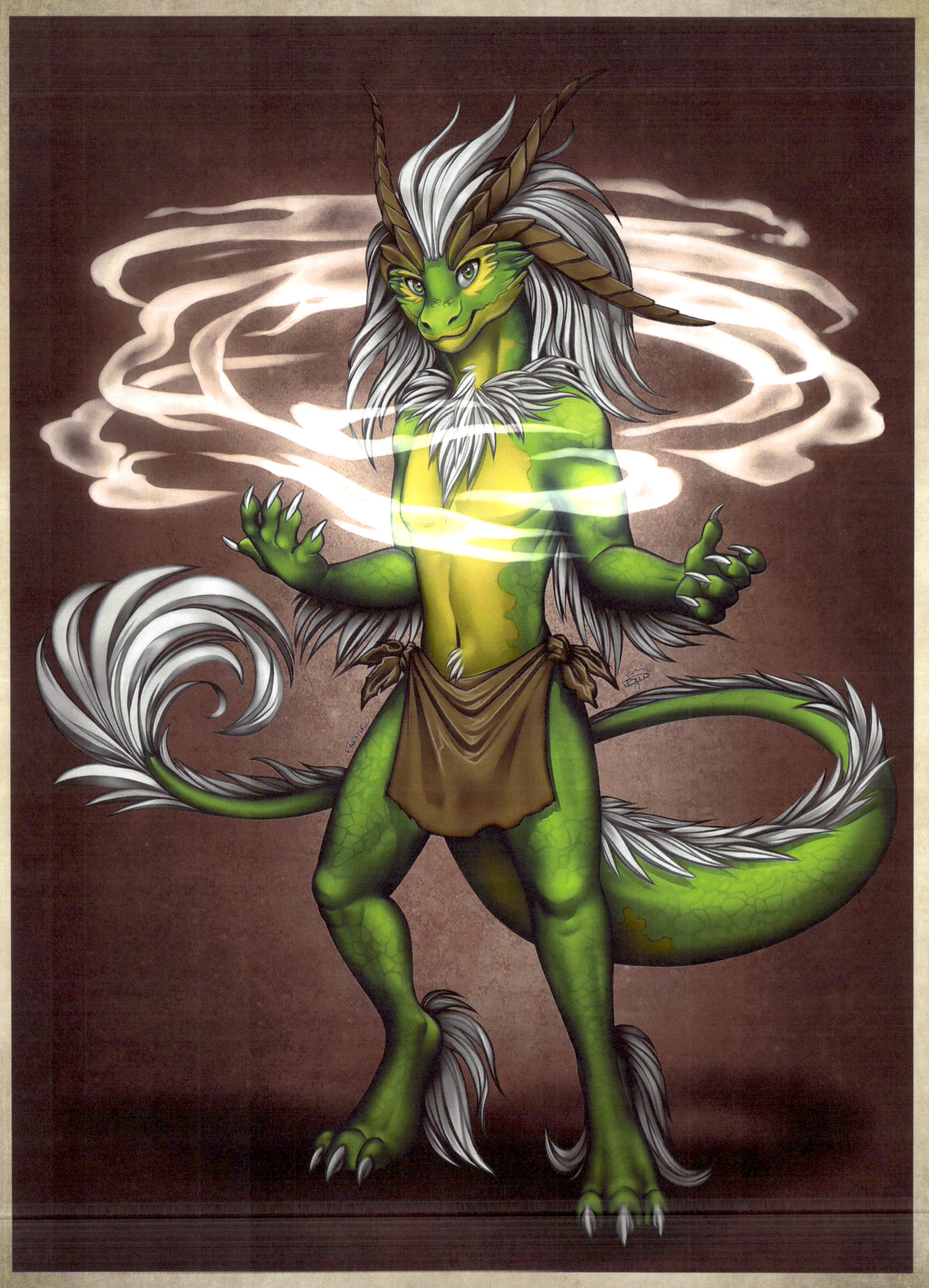

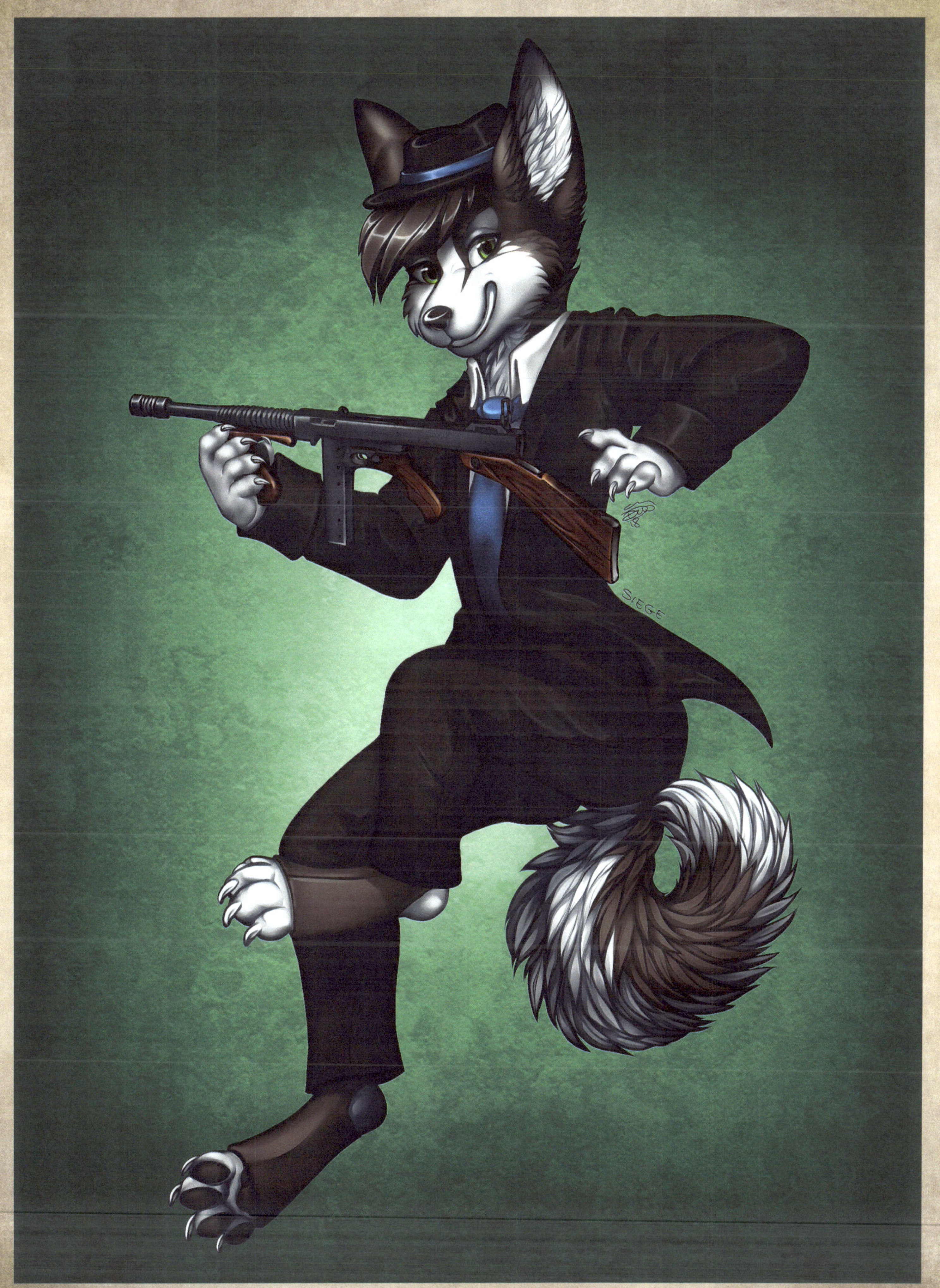
SIEGE

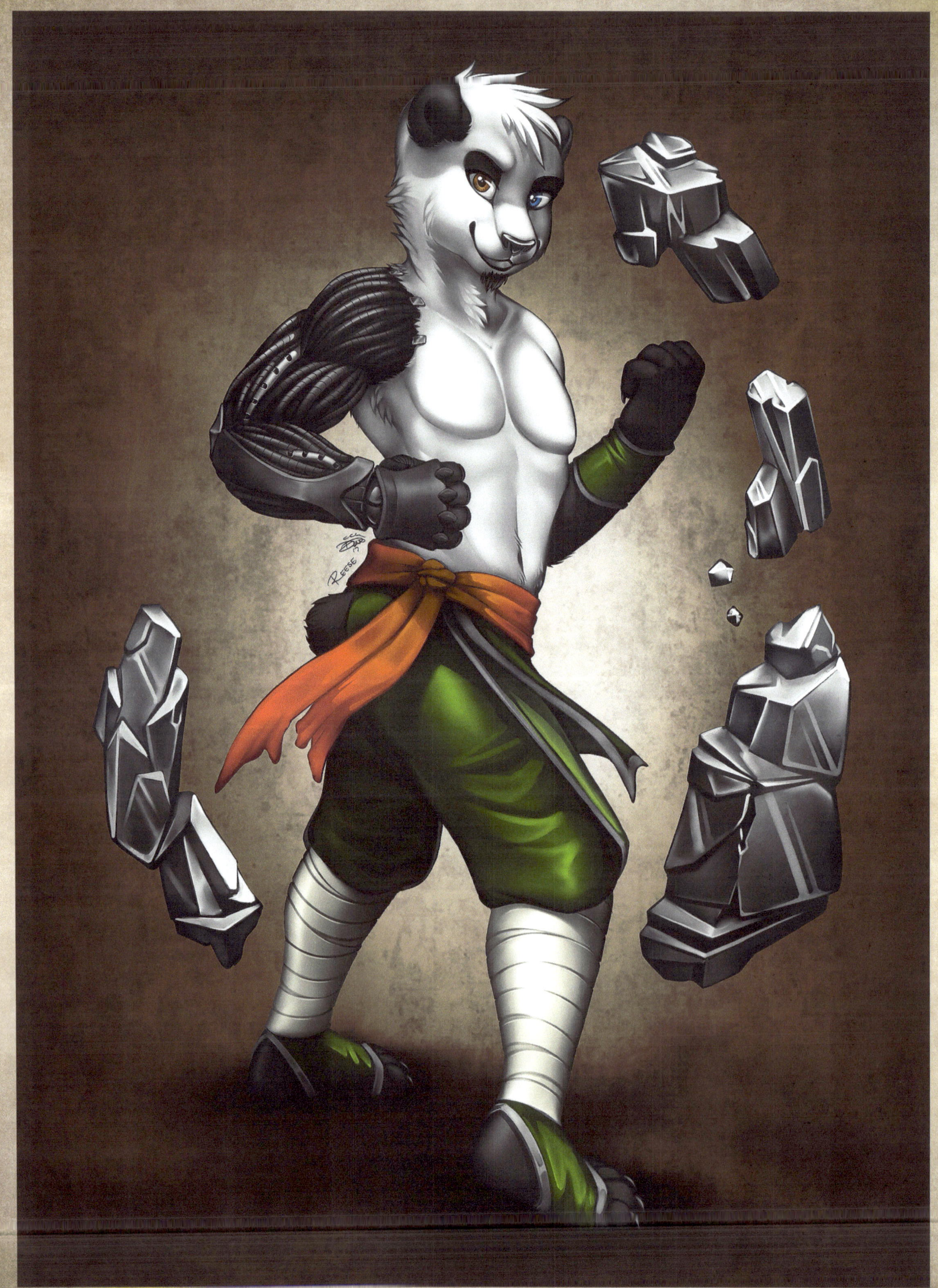
Reese

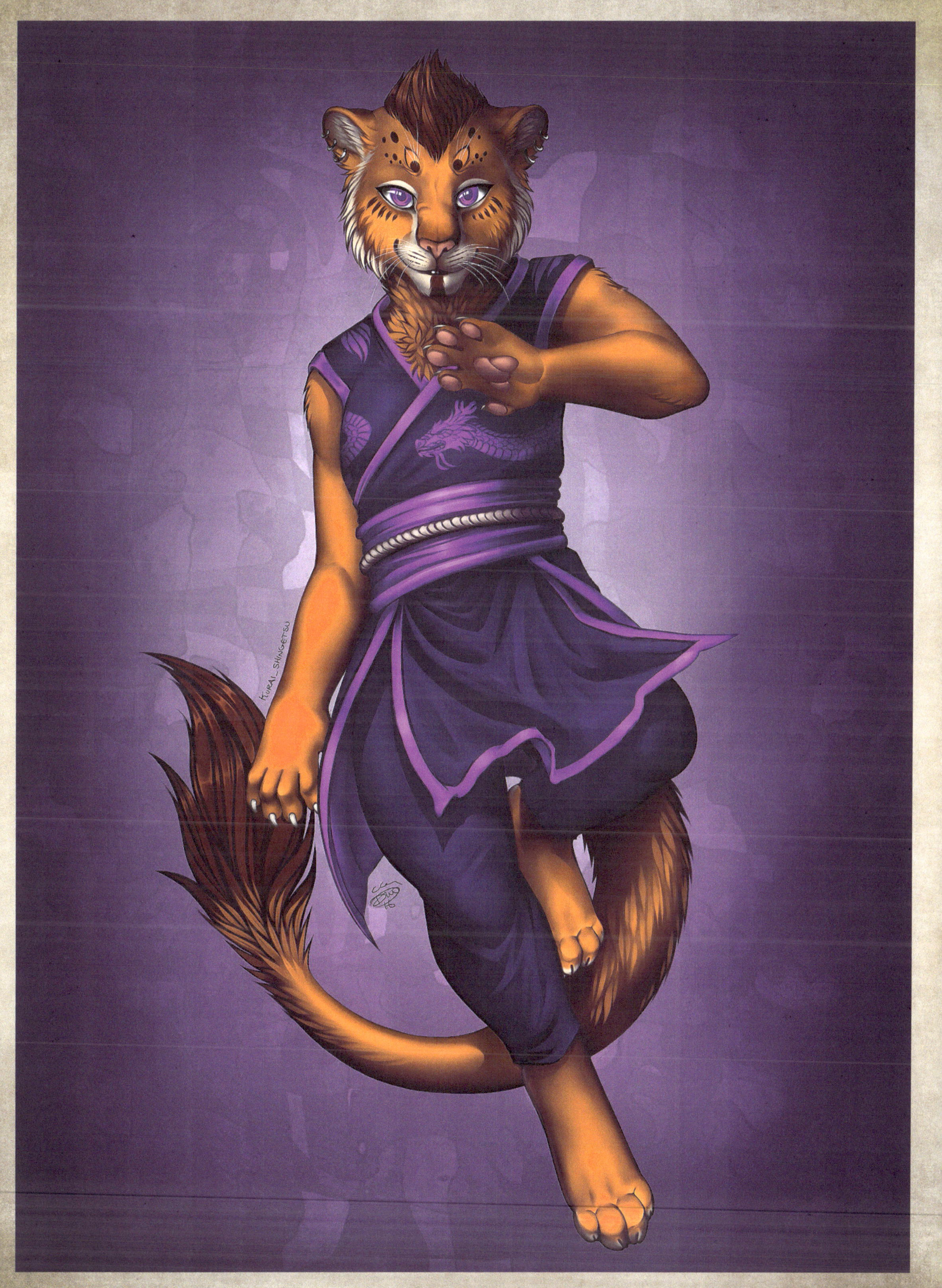
KURAI_SHINGETSU

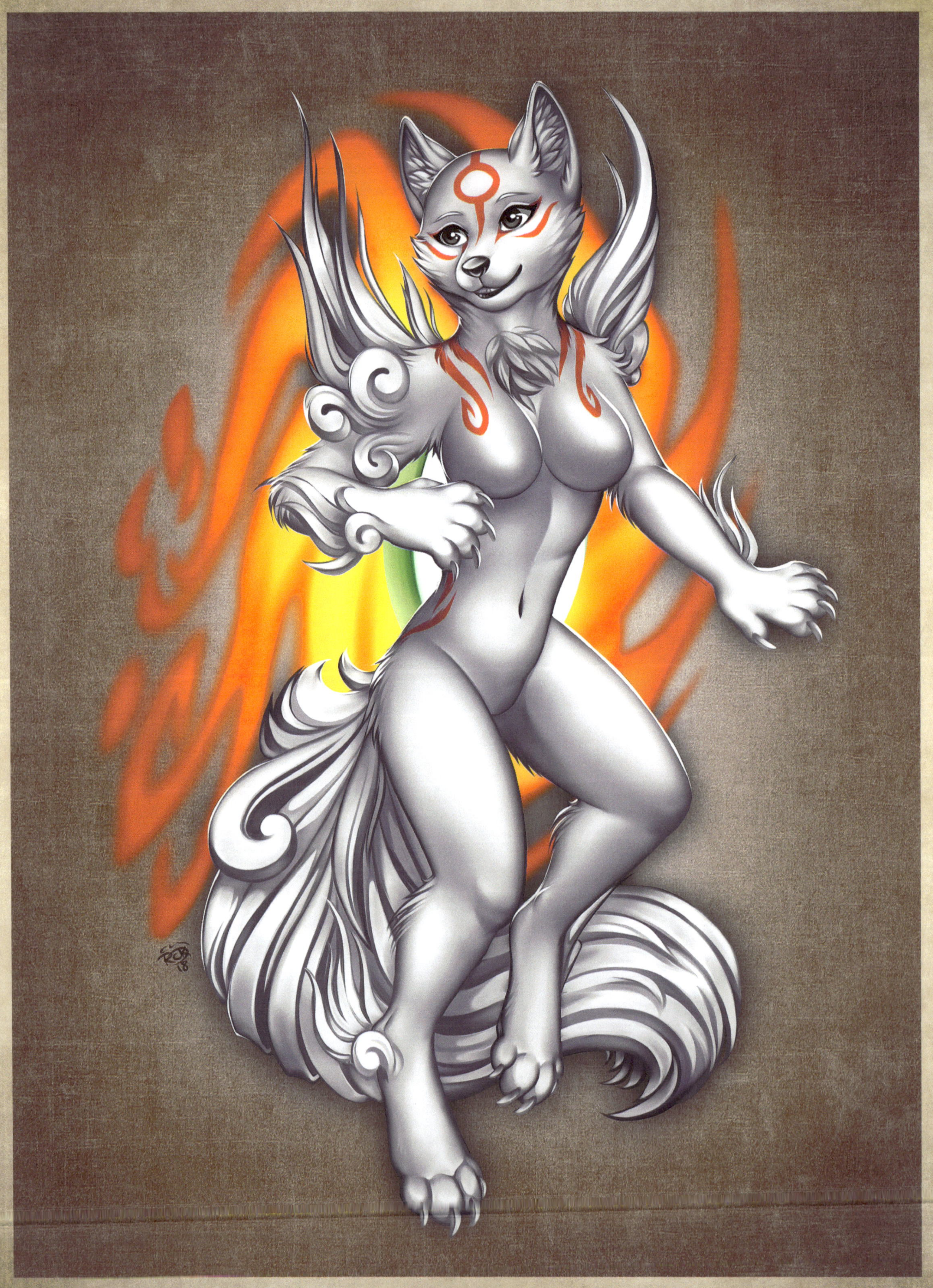

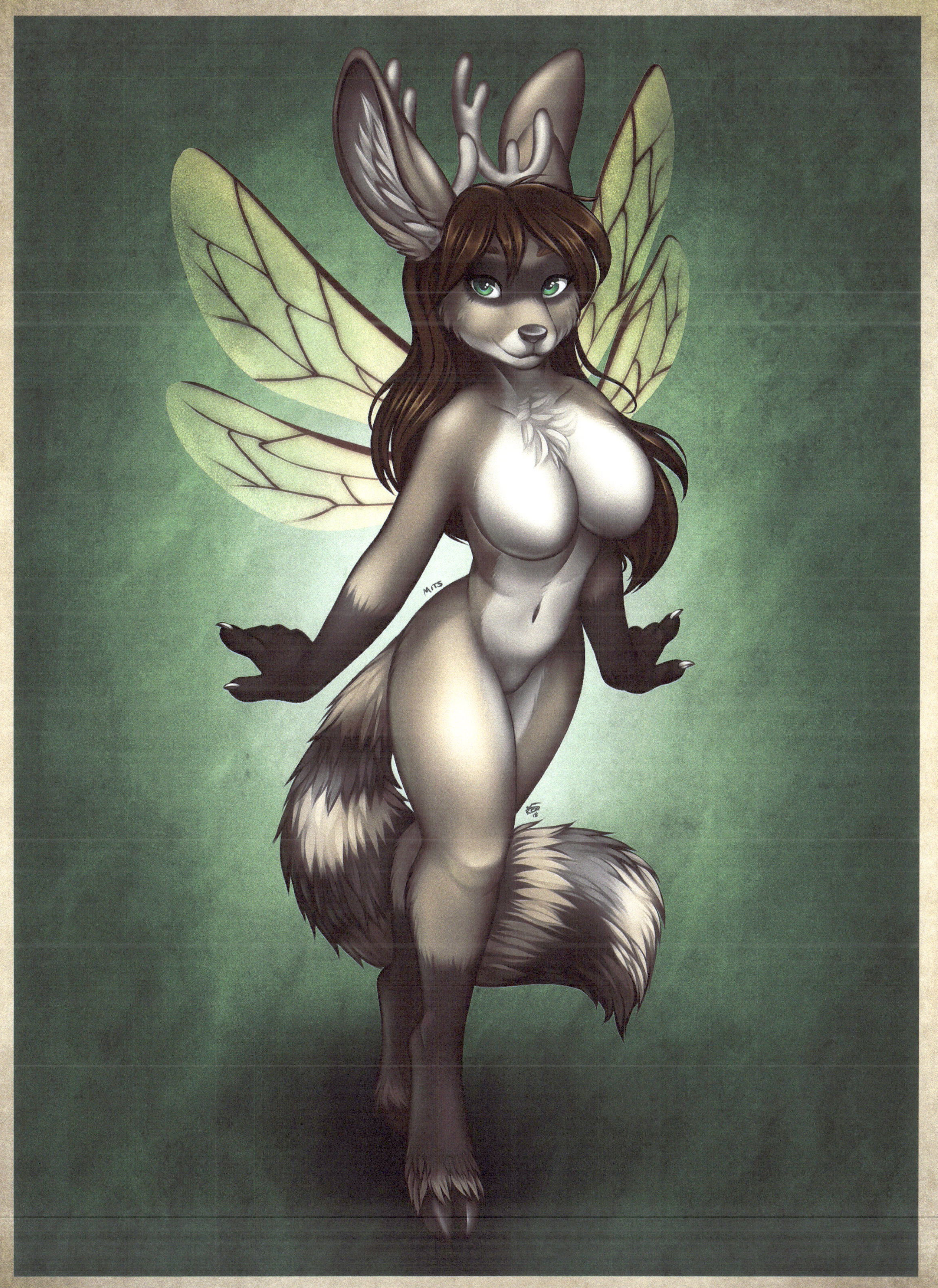
MITS

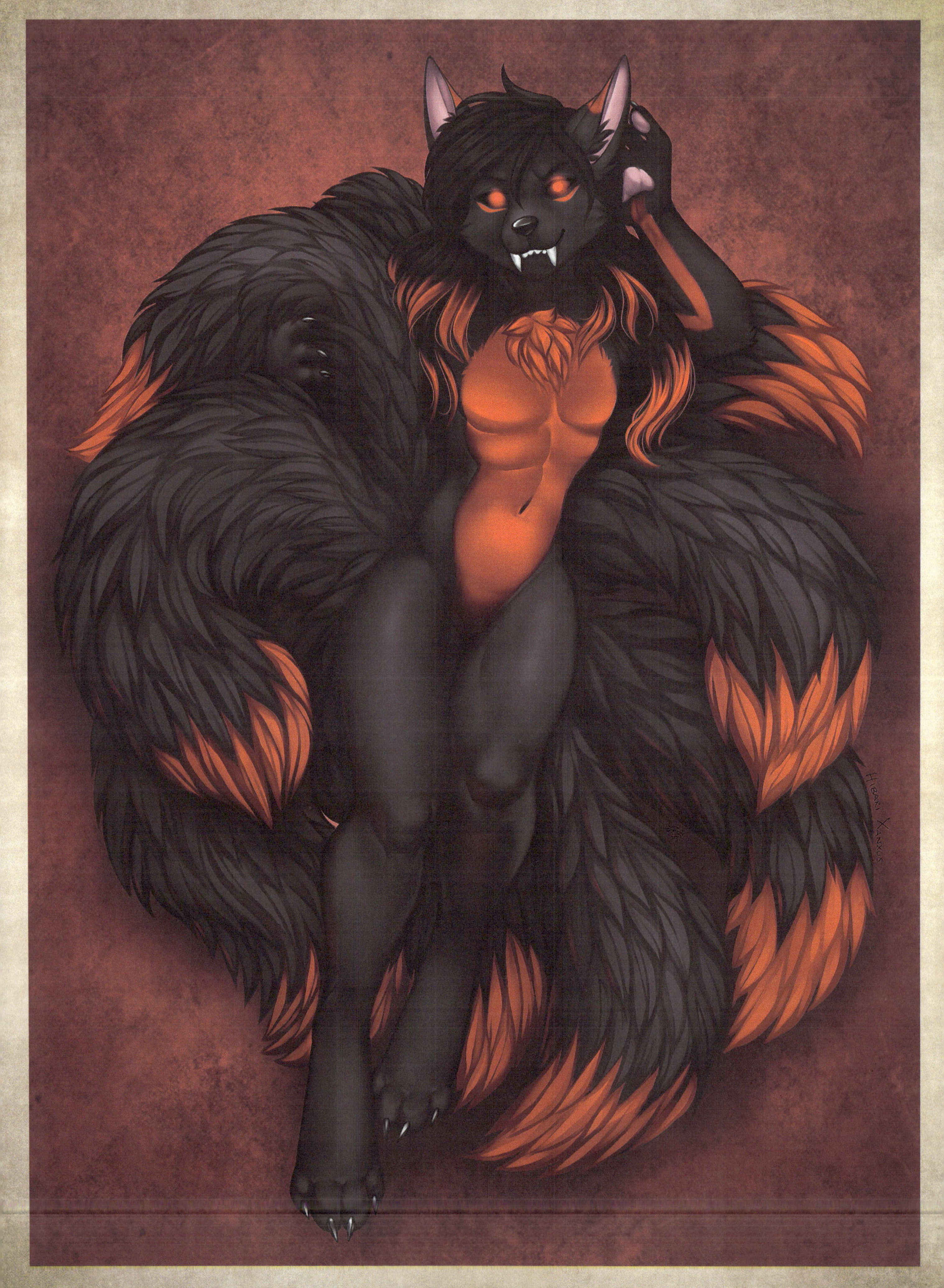
Hibari Xanxus

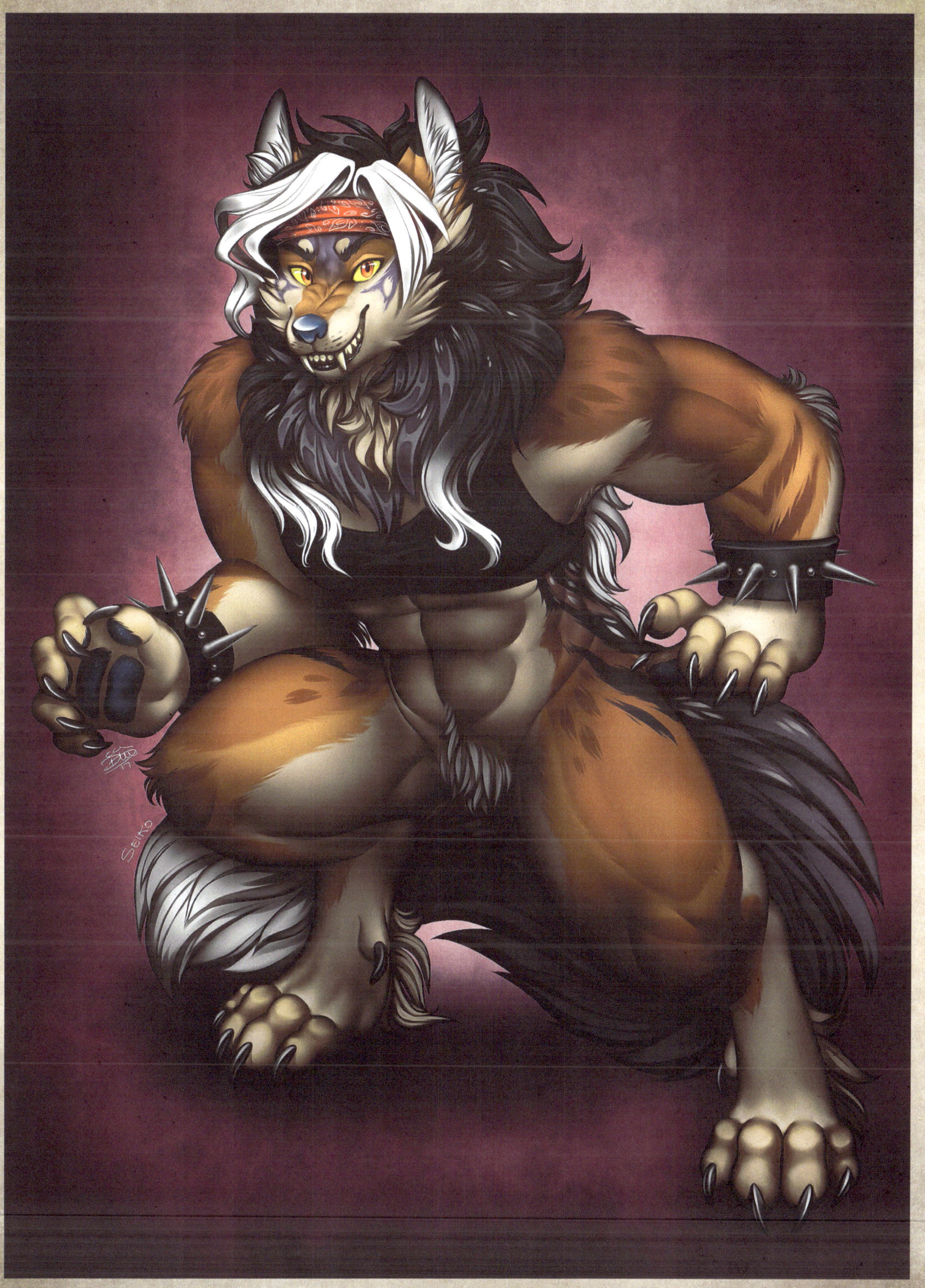
SEIKO

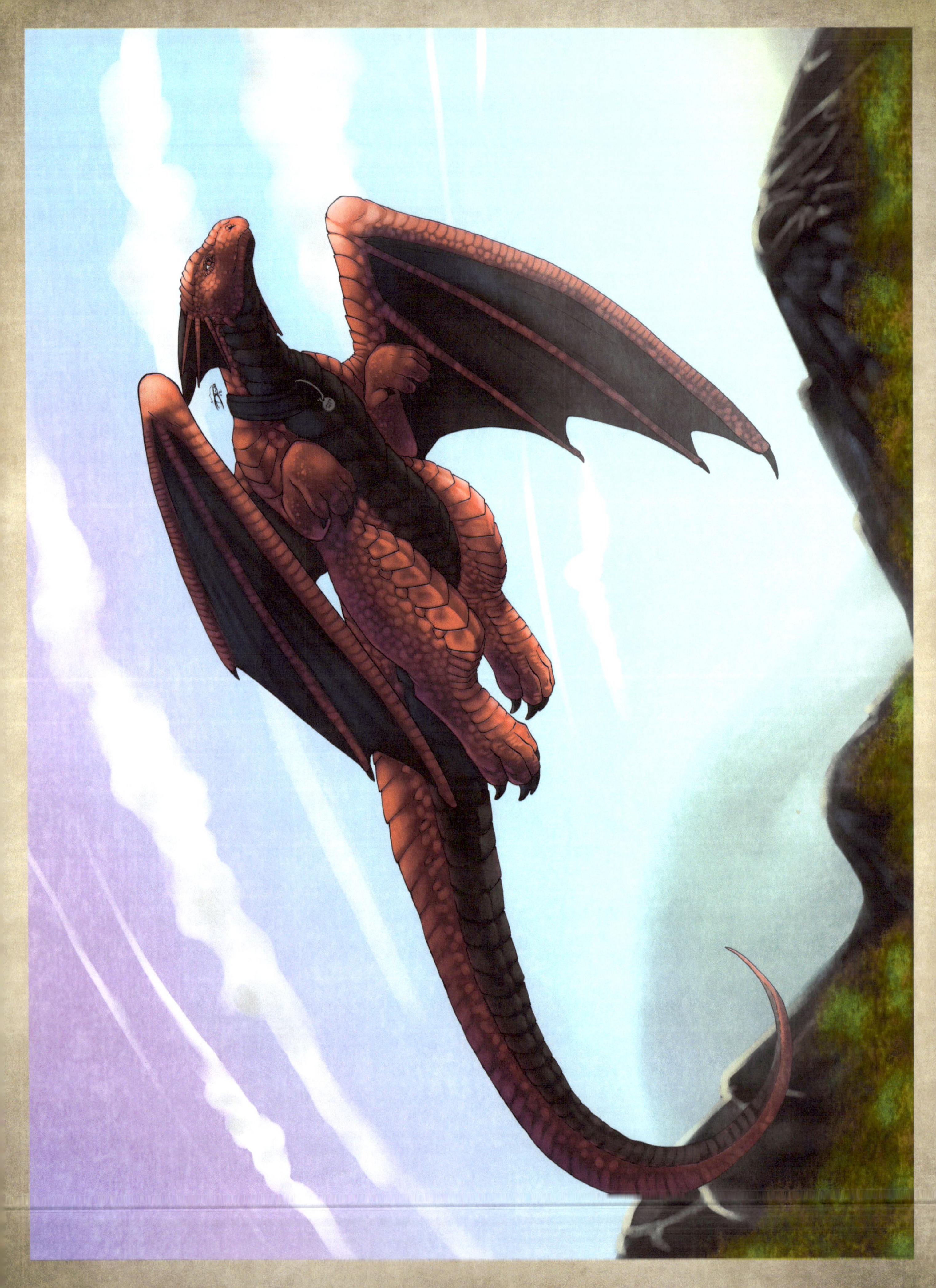

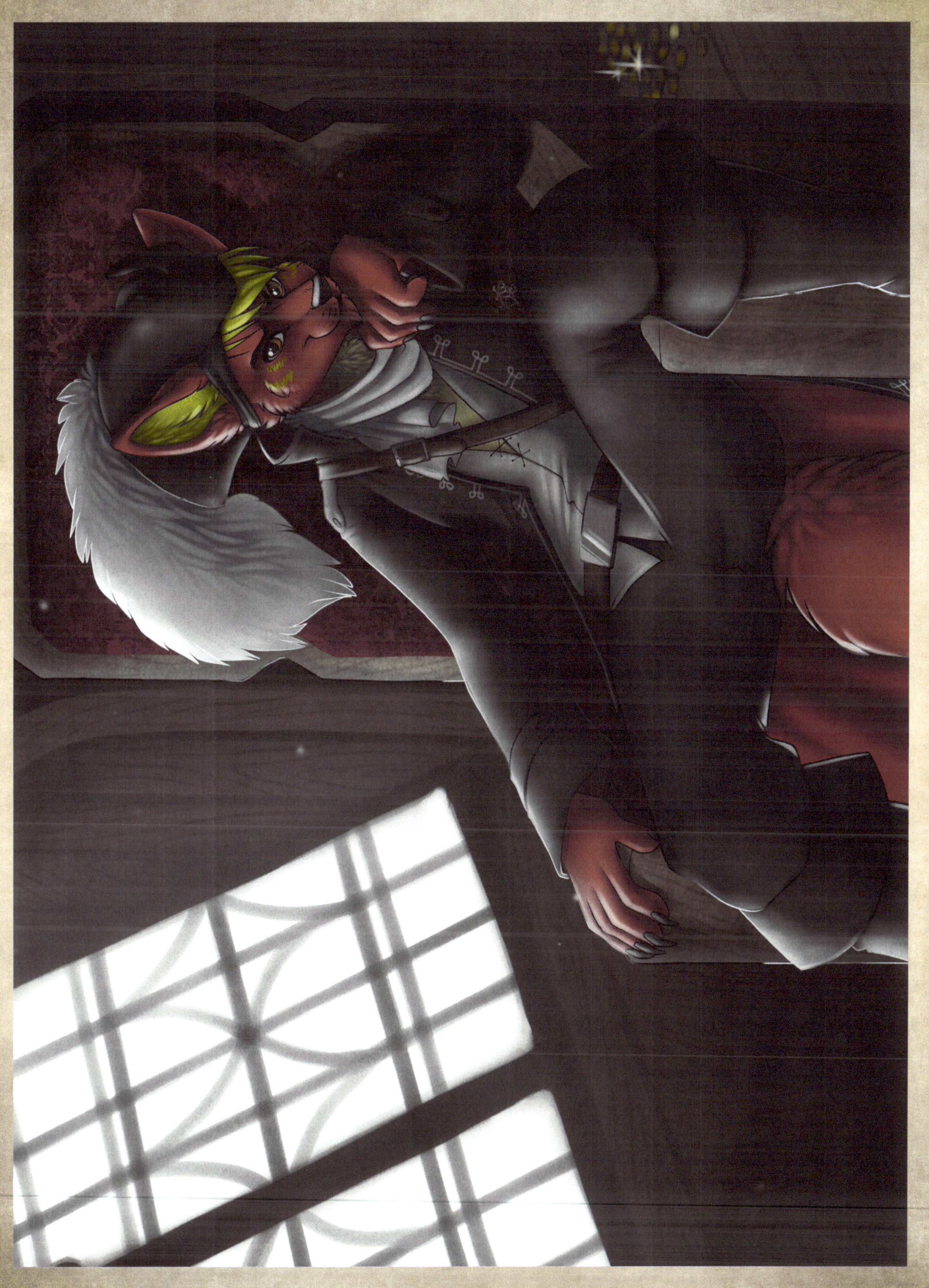

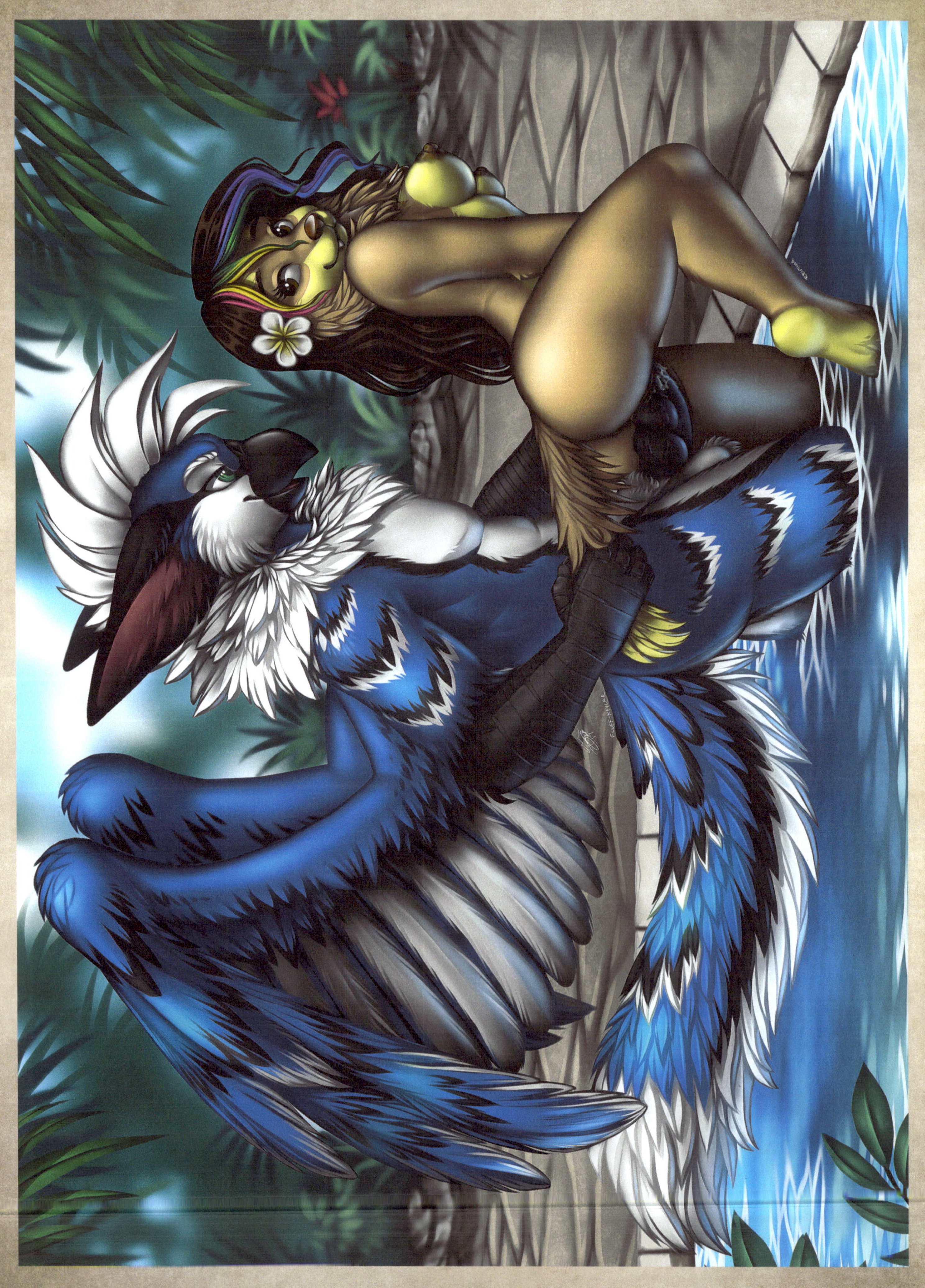

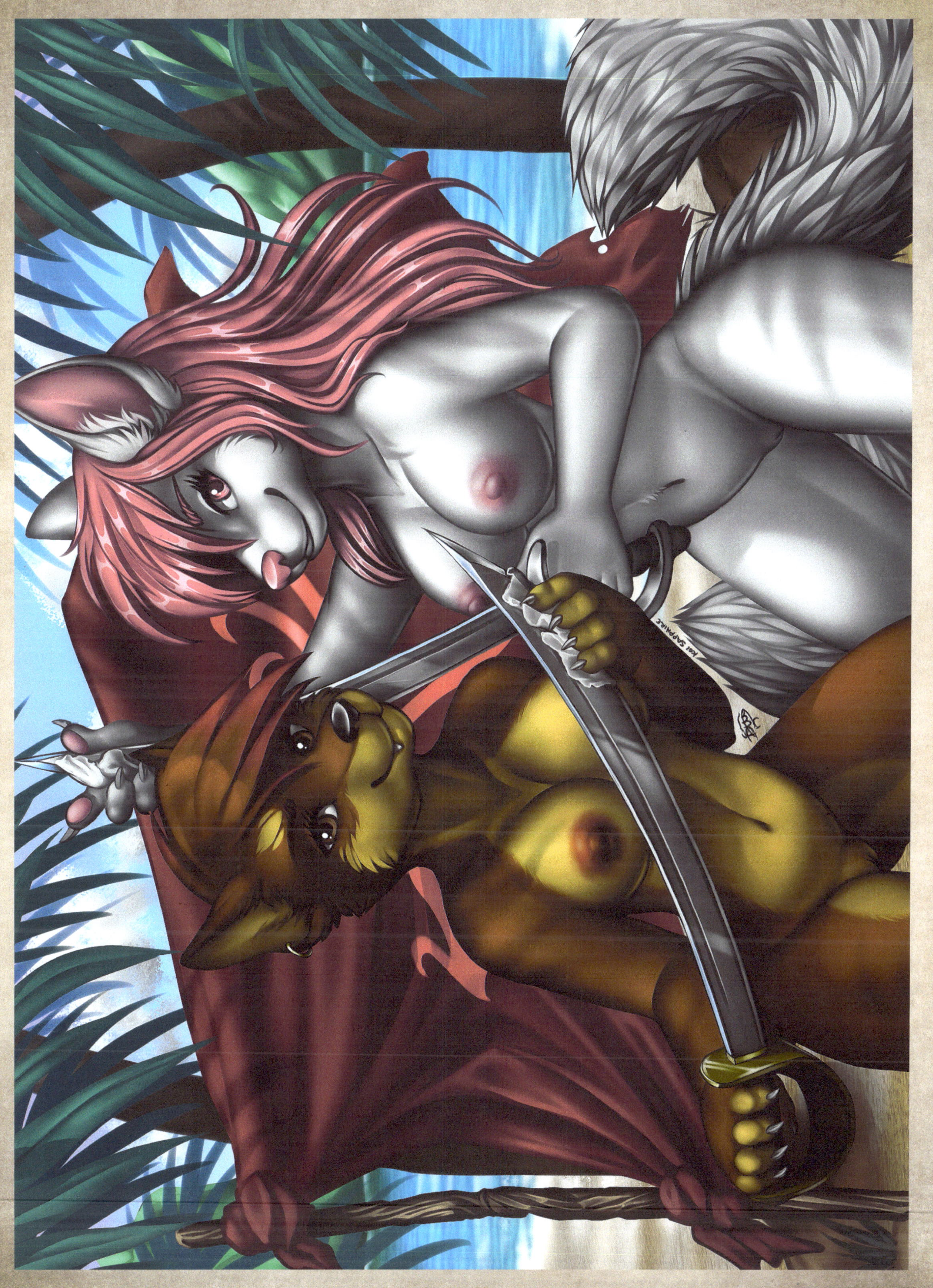

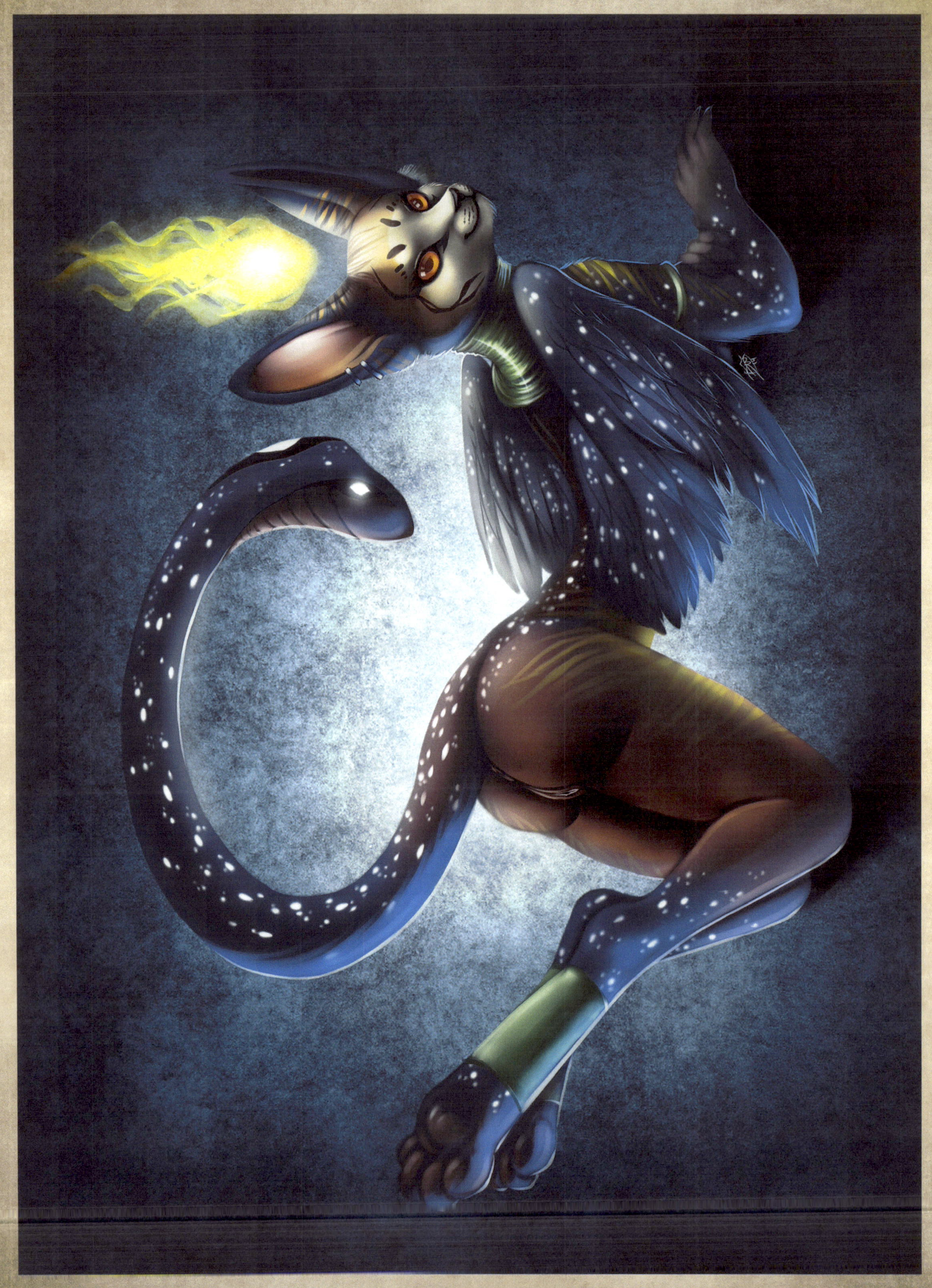

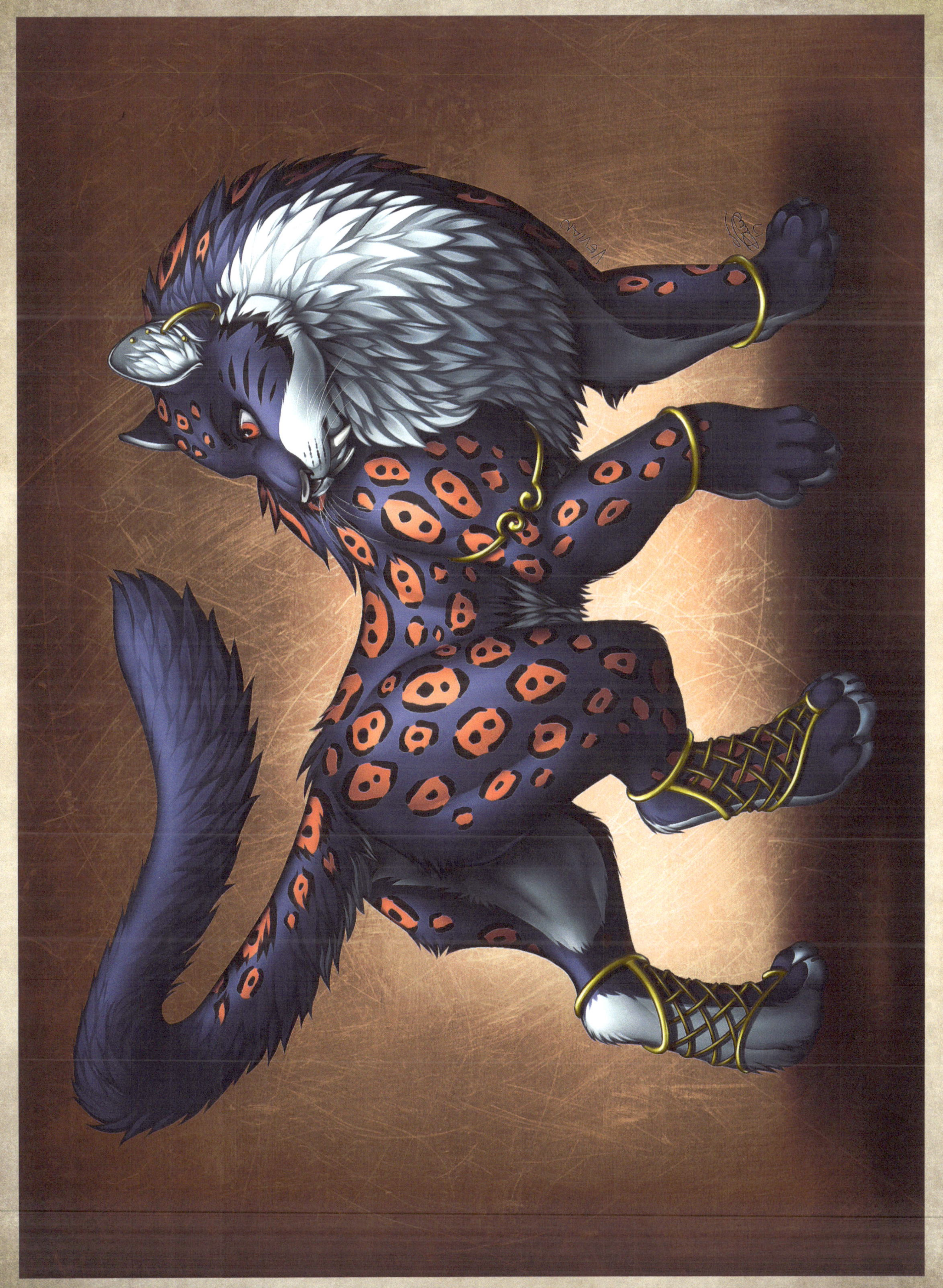

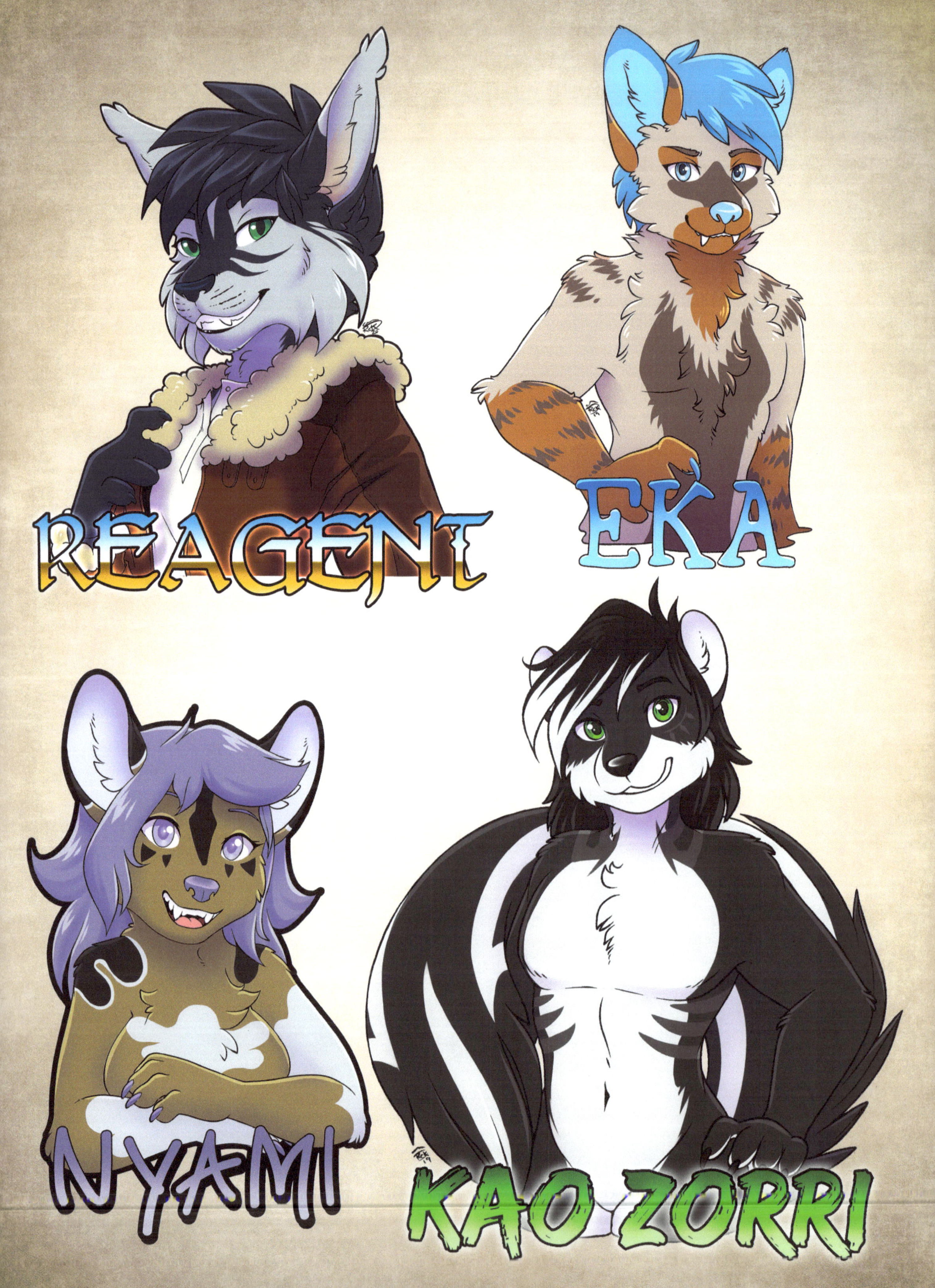
REAGENT
EKA
NYAMI
KAO ZORRI

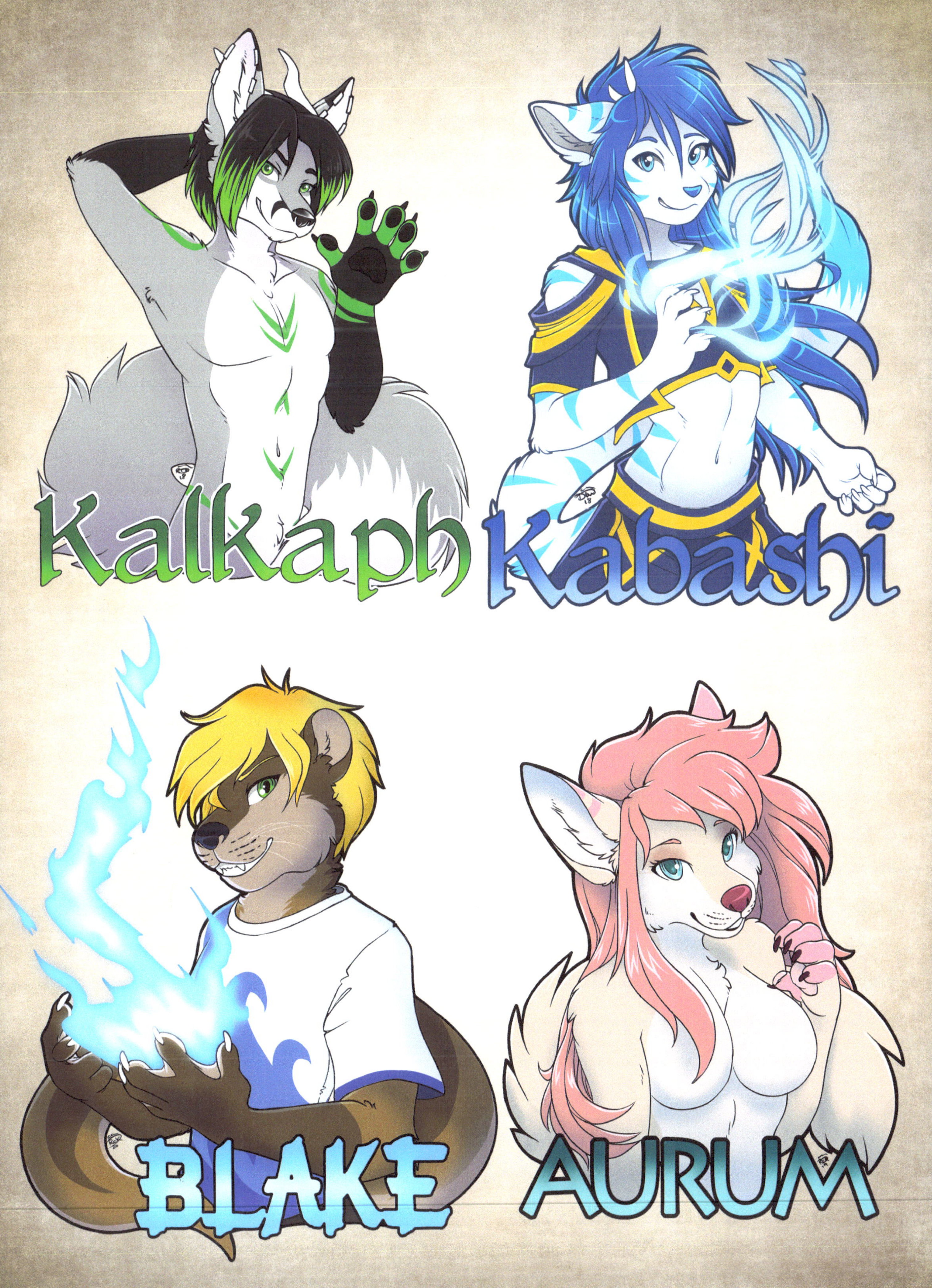
Kalkaph
Kabashi
BLAKE
AURUM

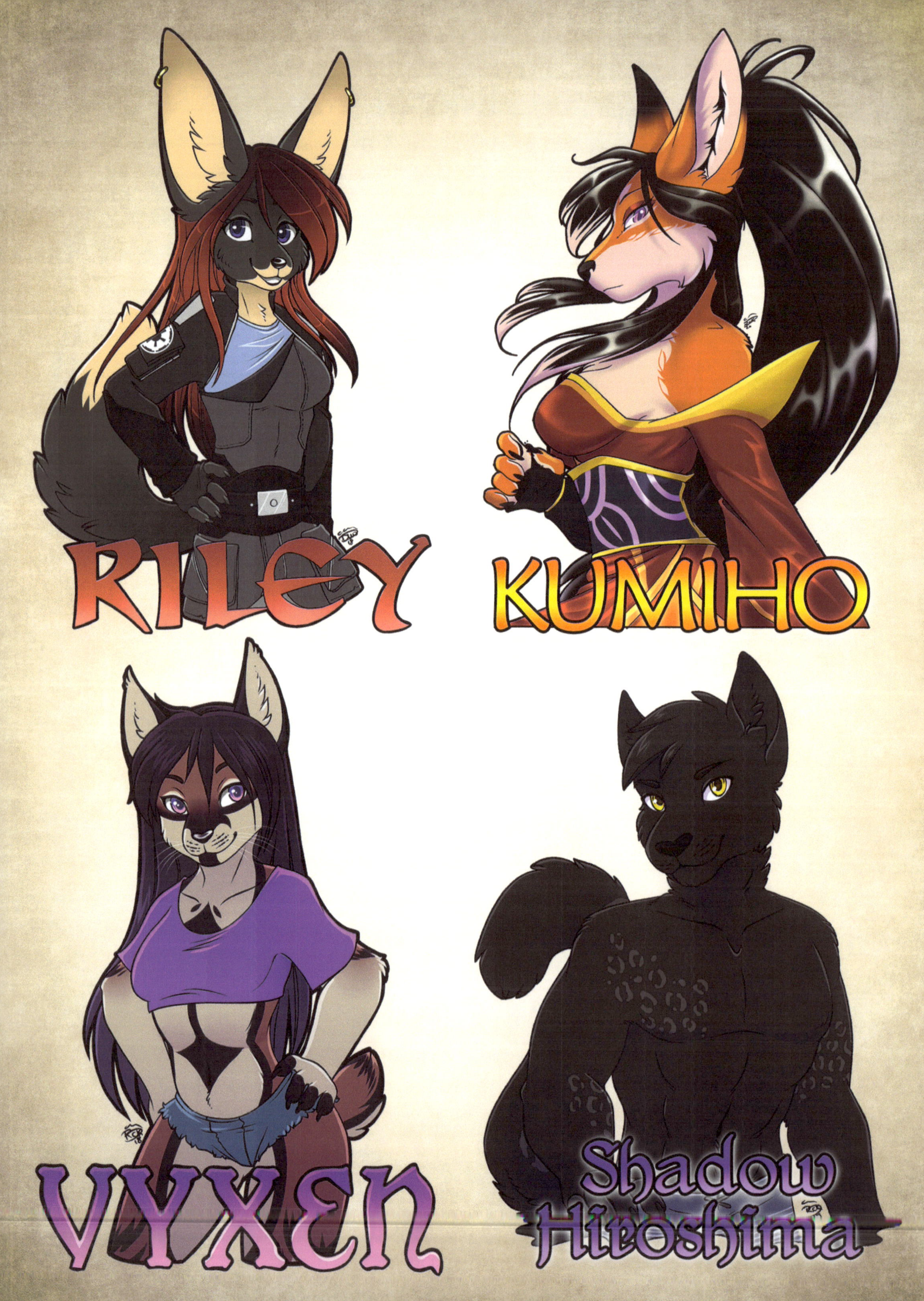

RILEY
KUMIHO
VYXEN
Shadow
Hiroshima

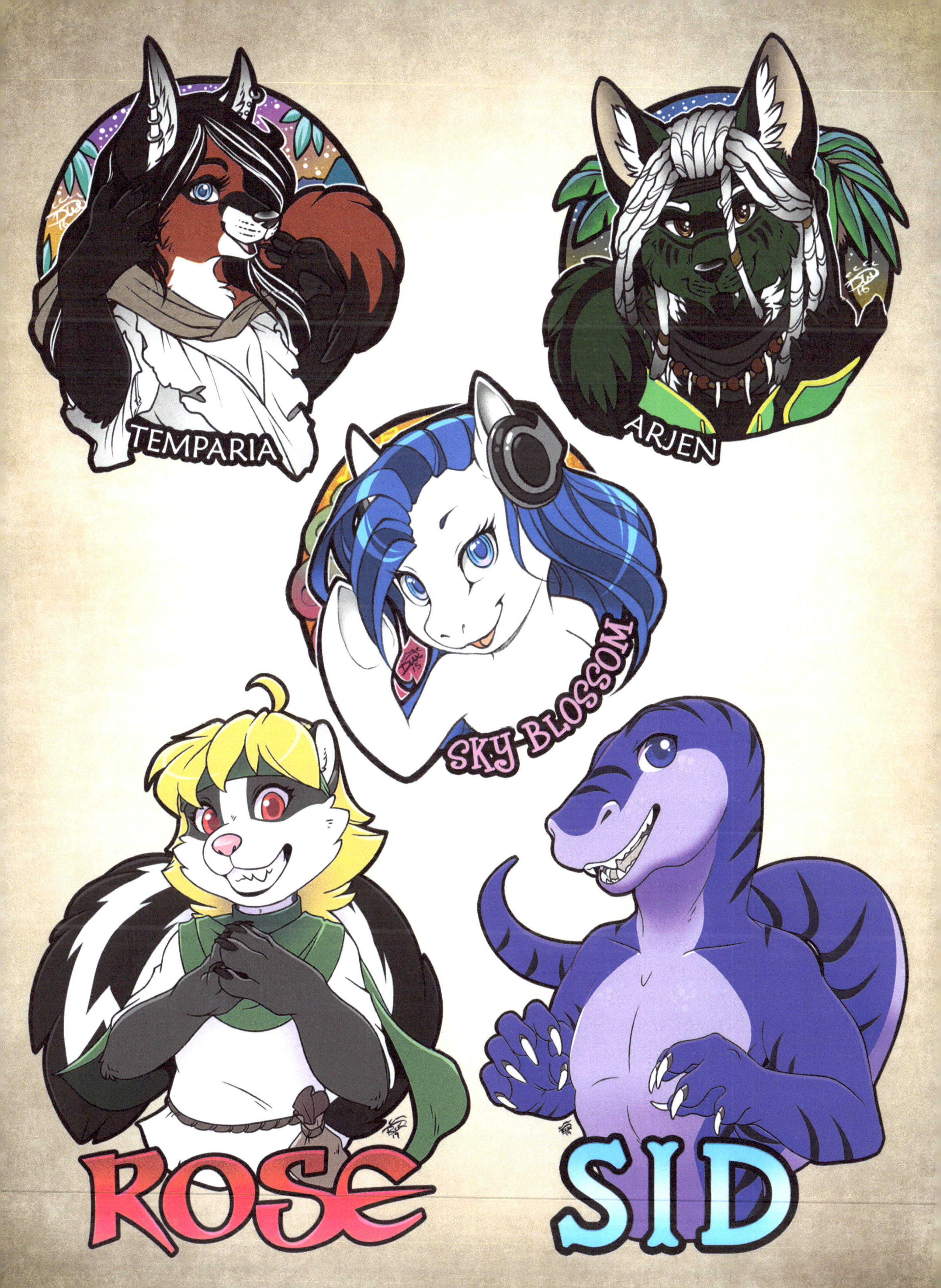
TEMPARIA
ARJEN
SKY BLOSSOM
ROSE
SID

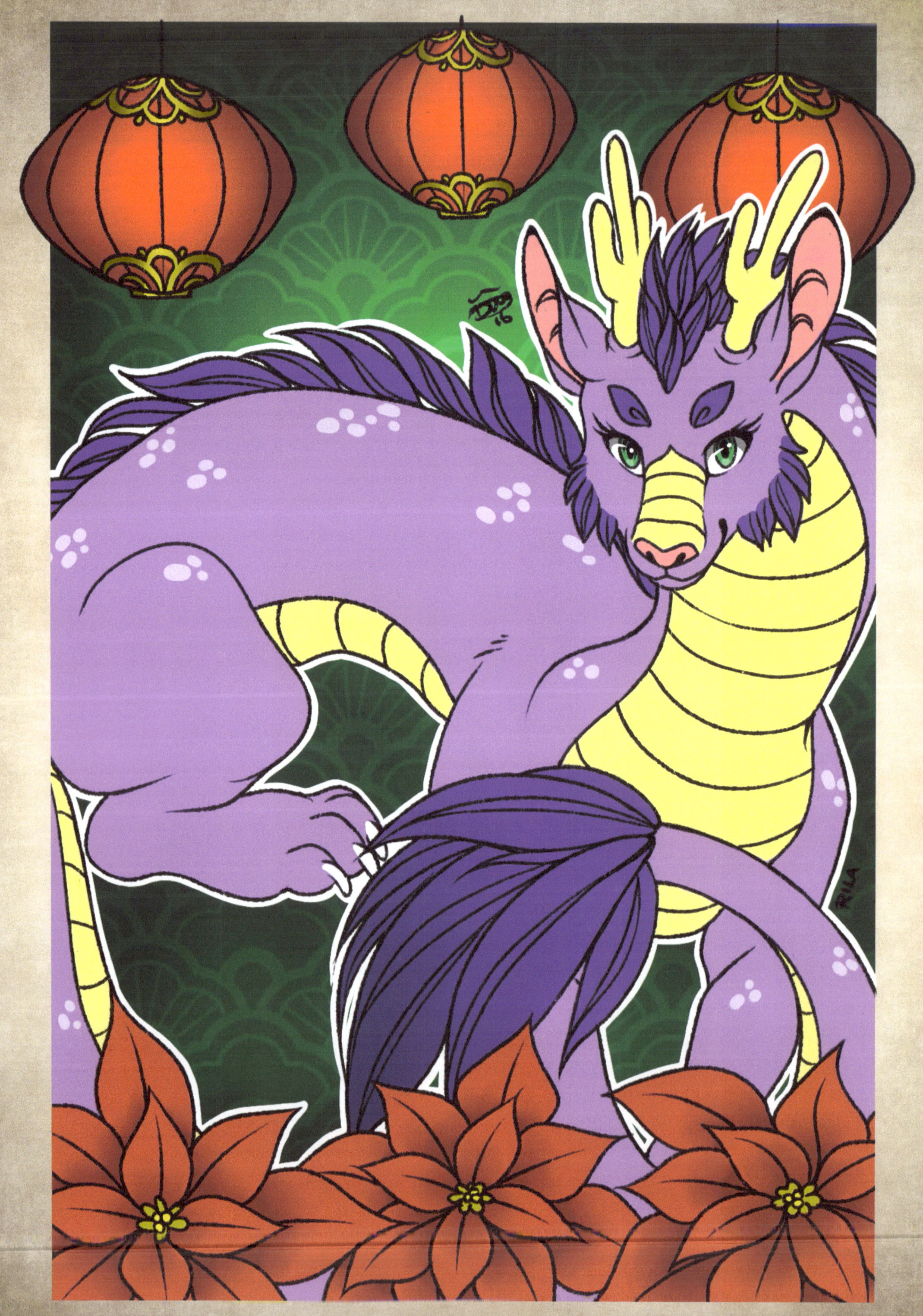

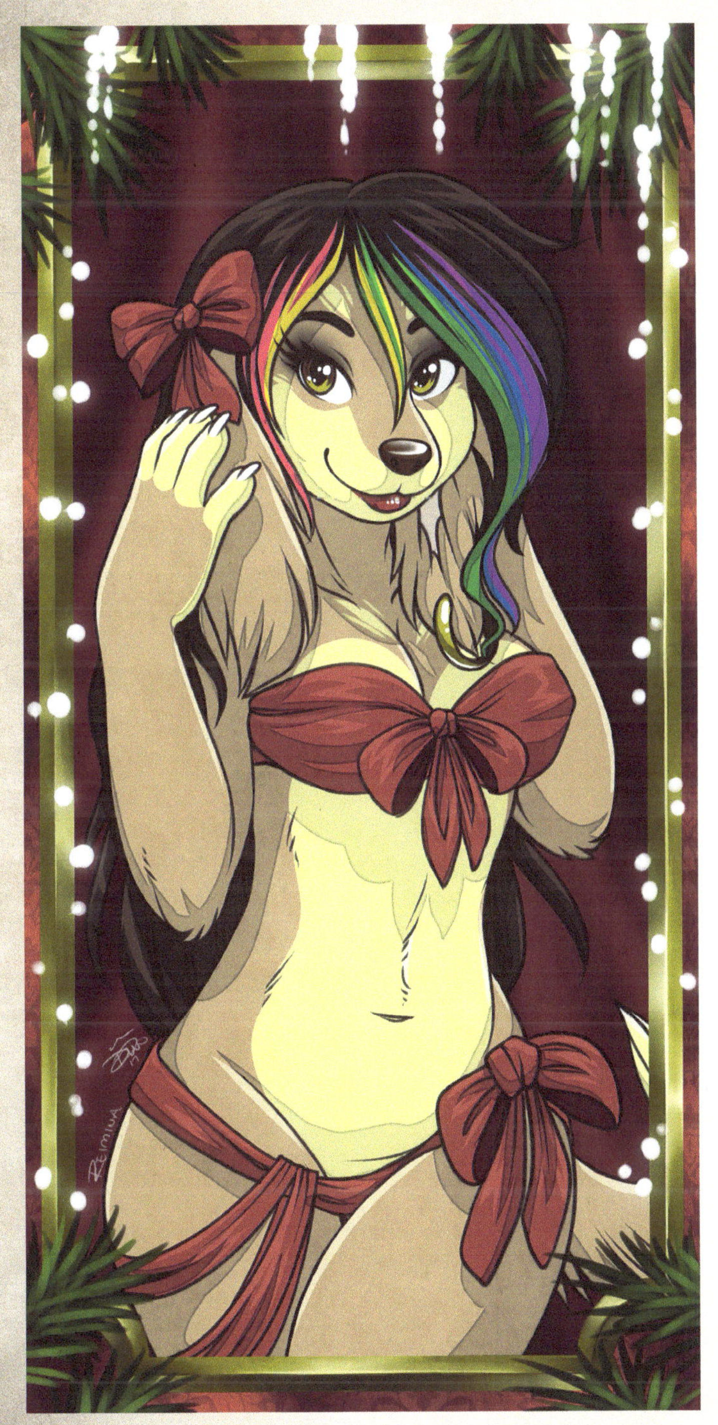
REIMINA

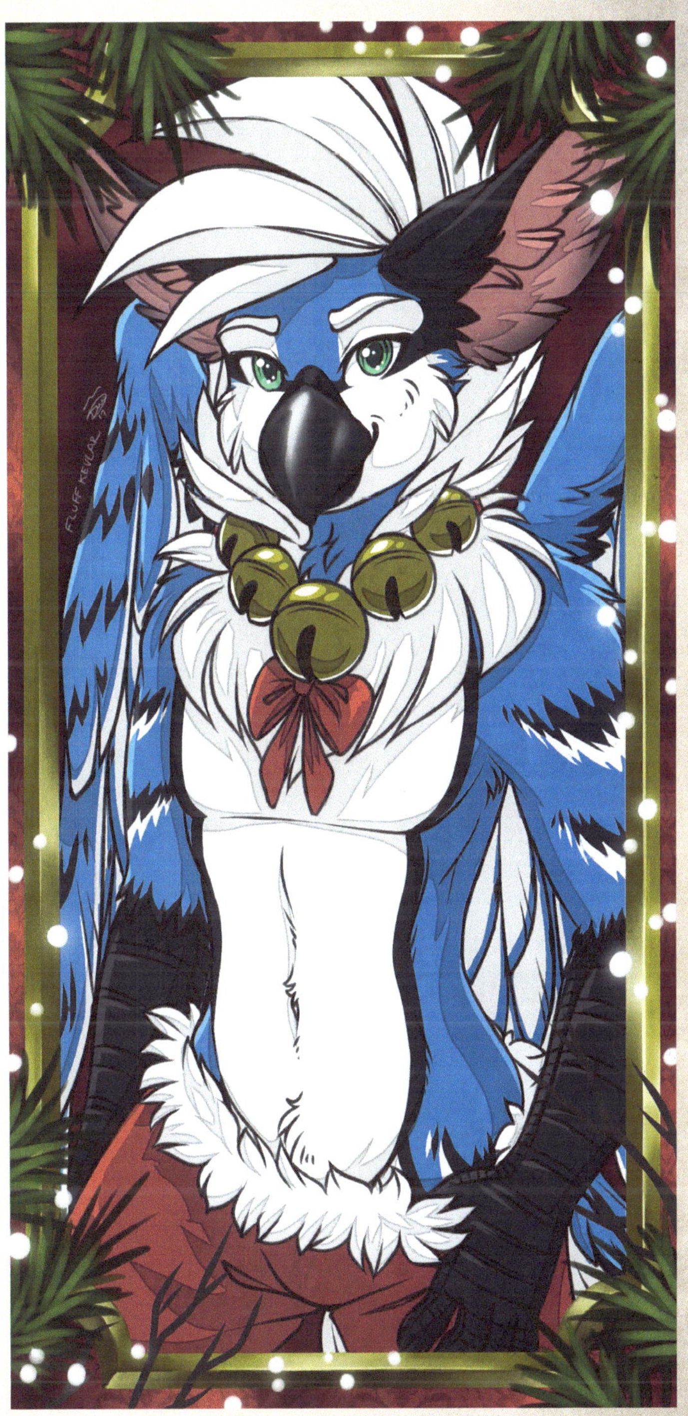
FLUFF KEVLAR

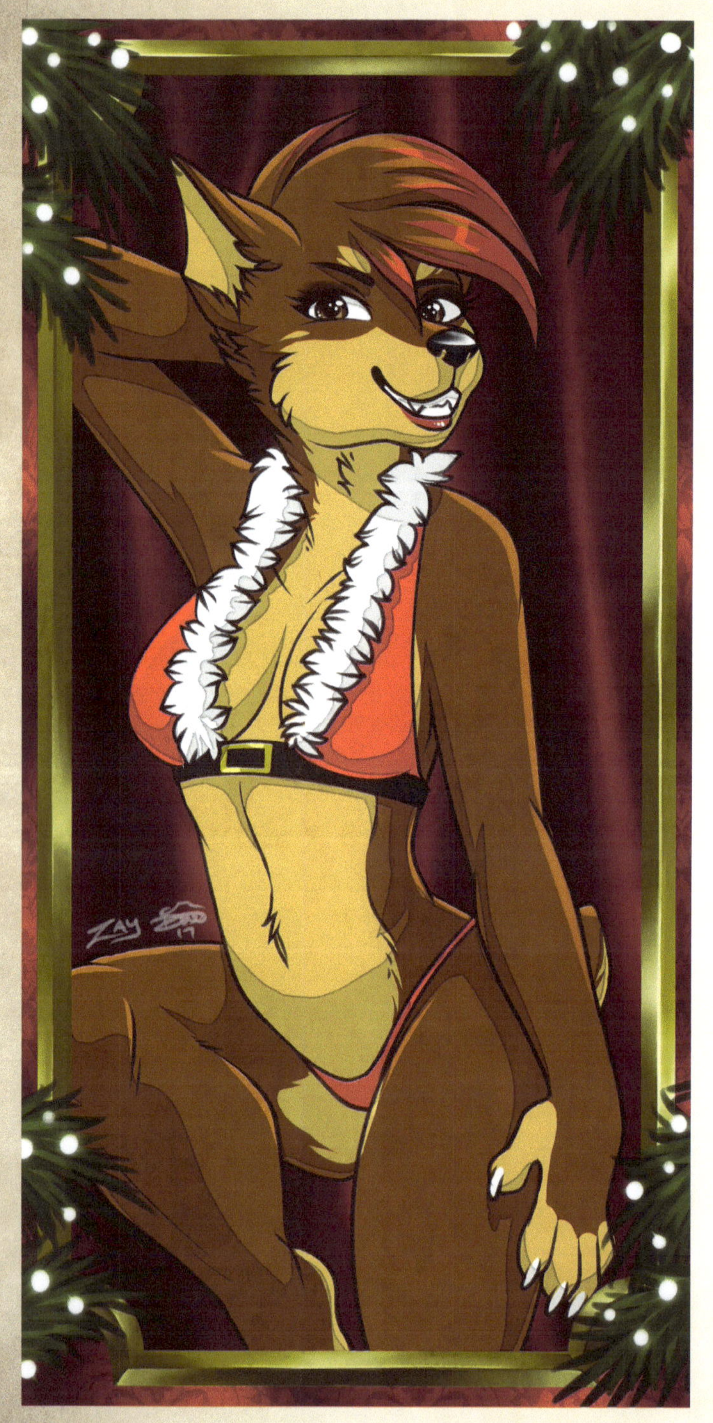

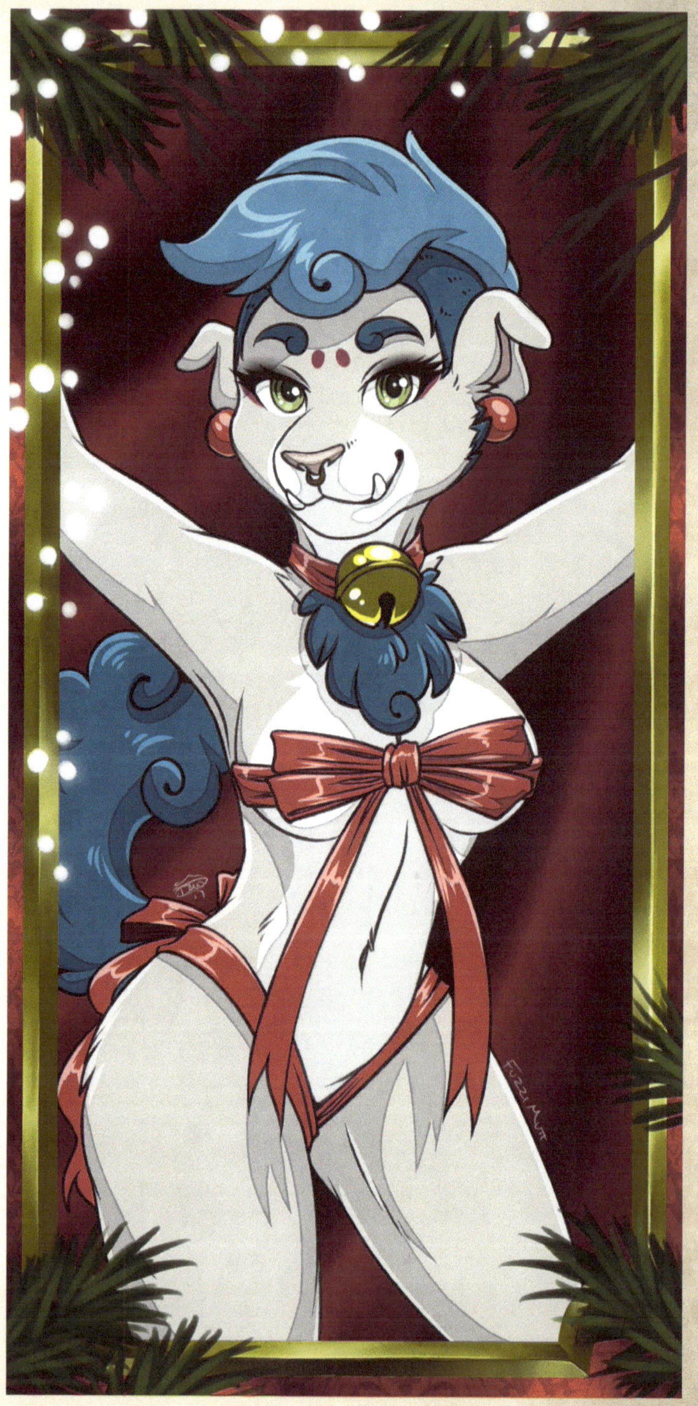

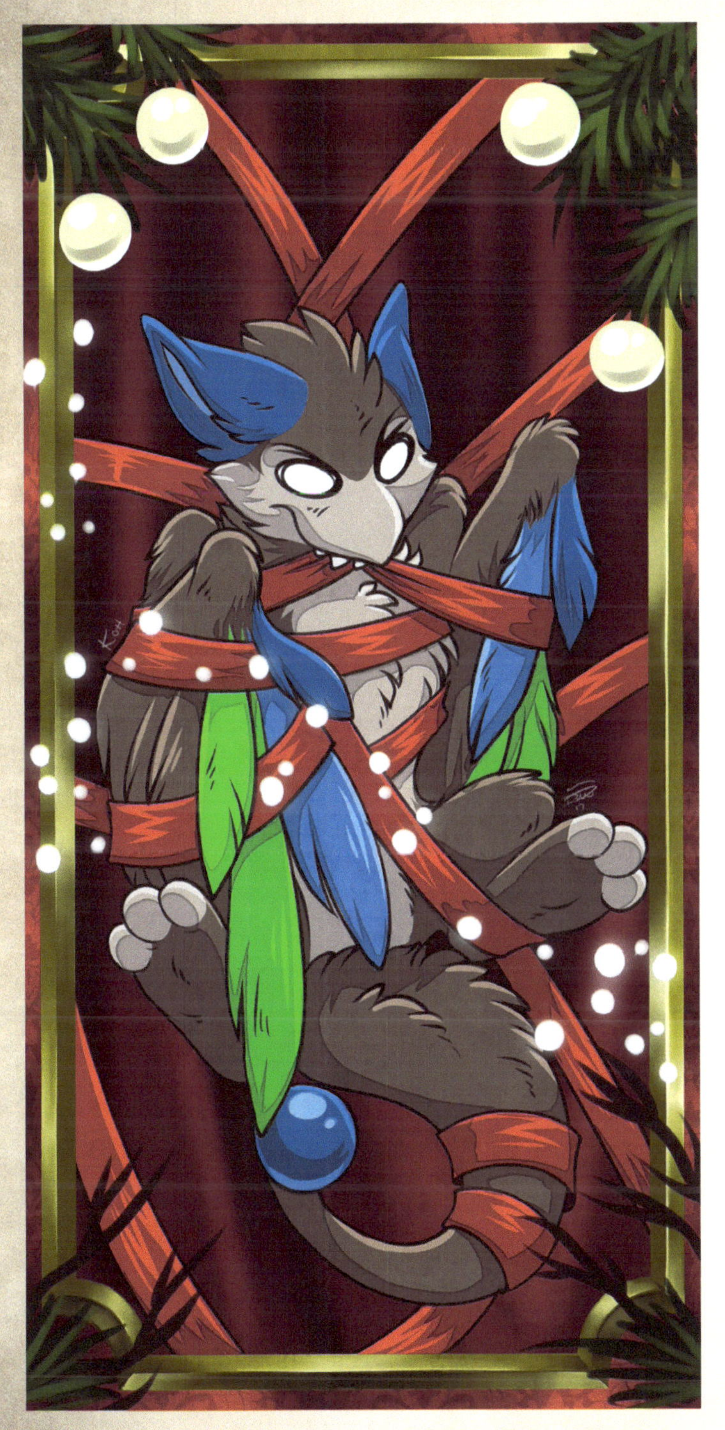

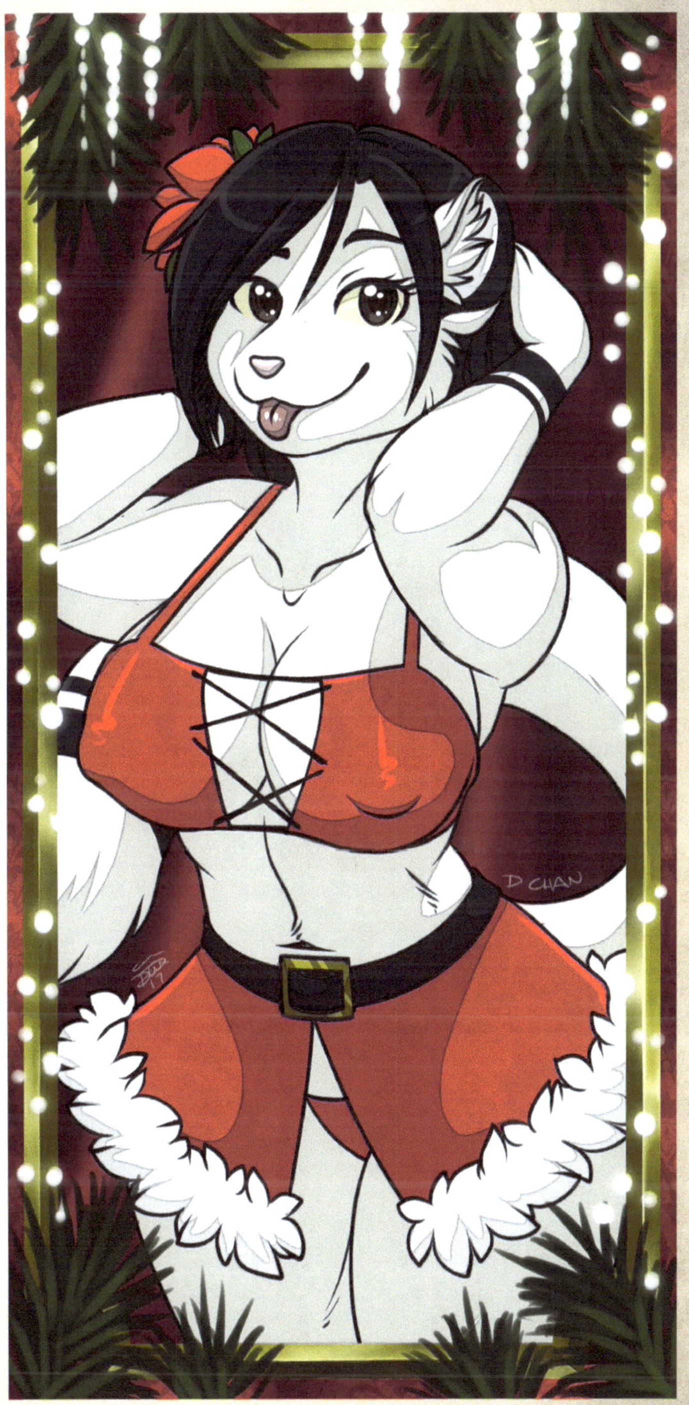

D CHAN

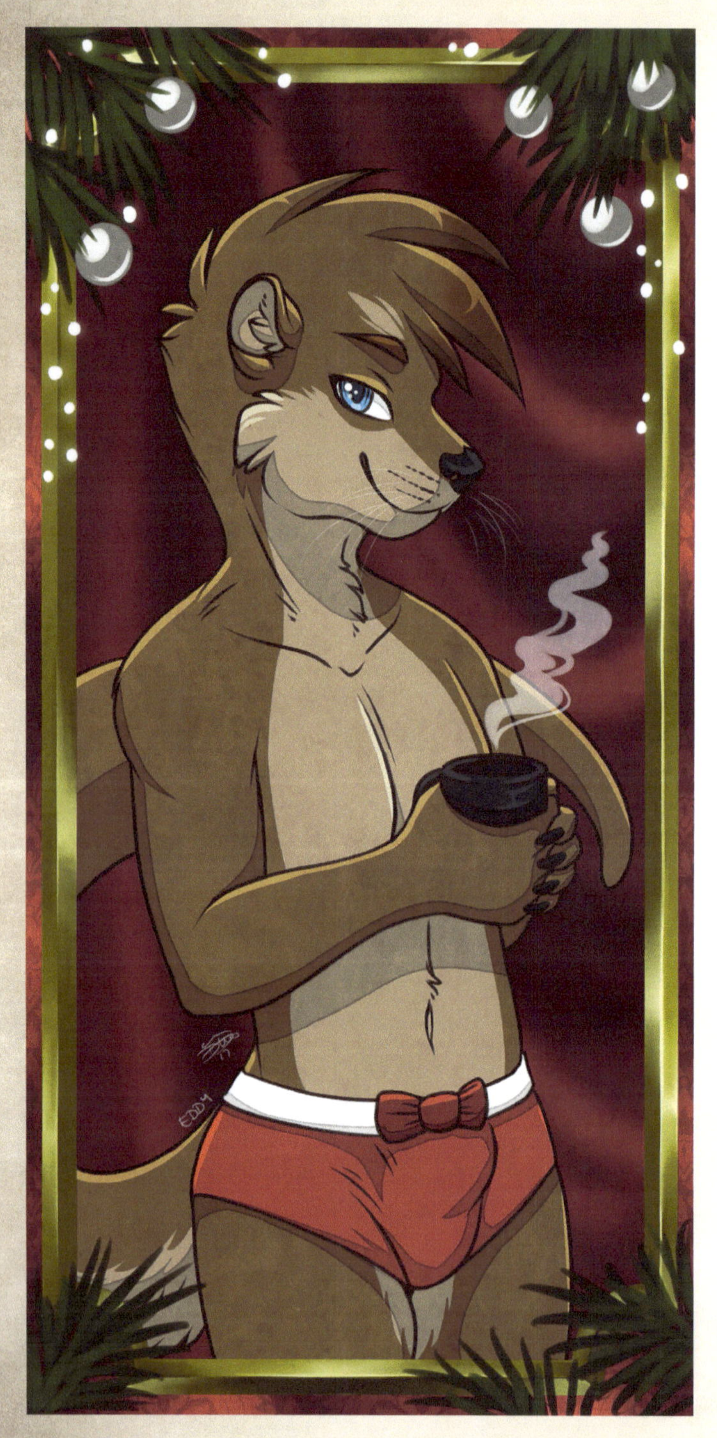

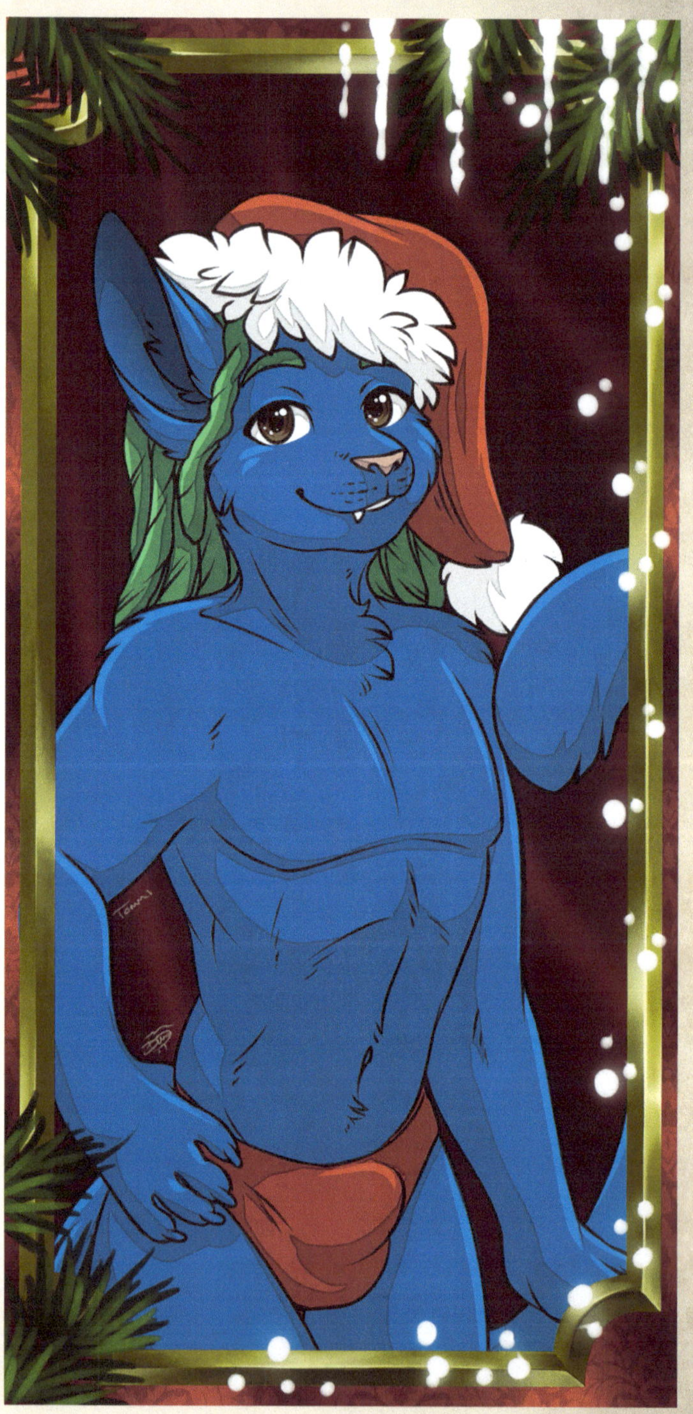

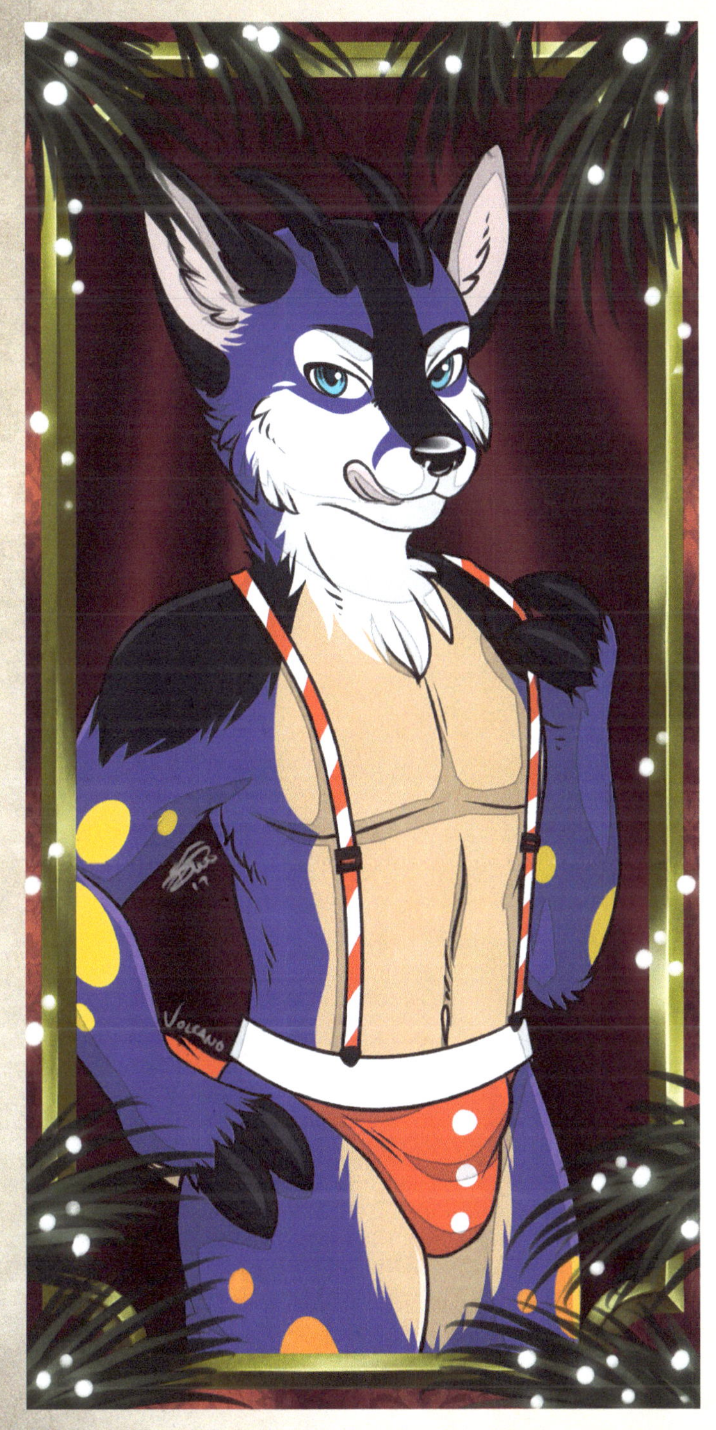

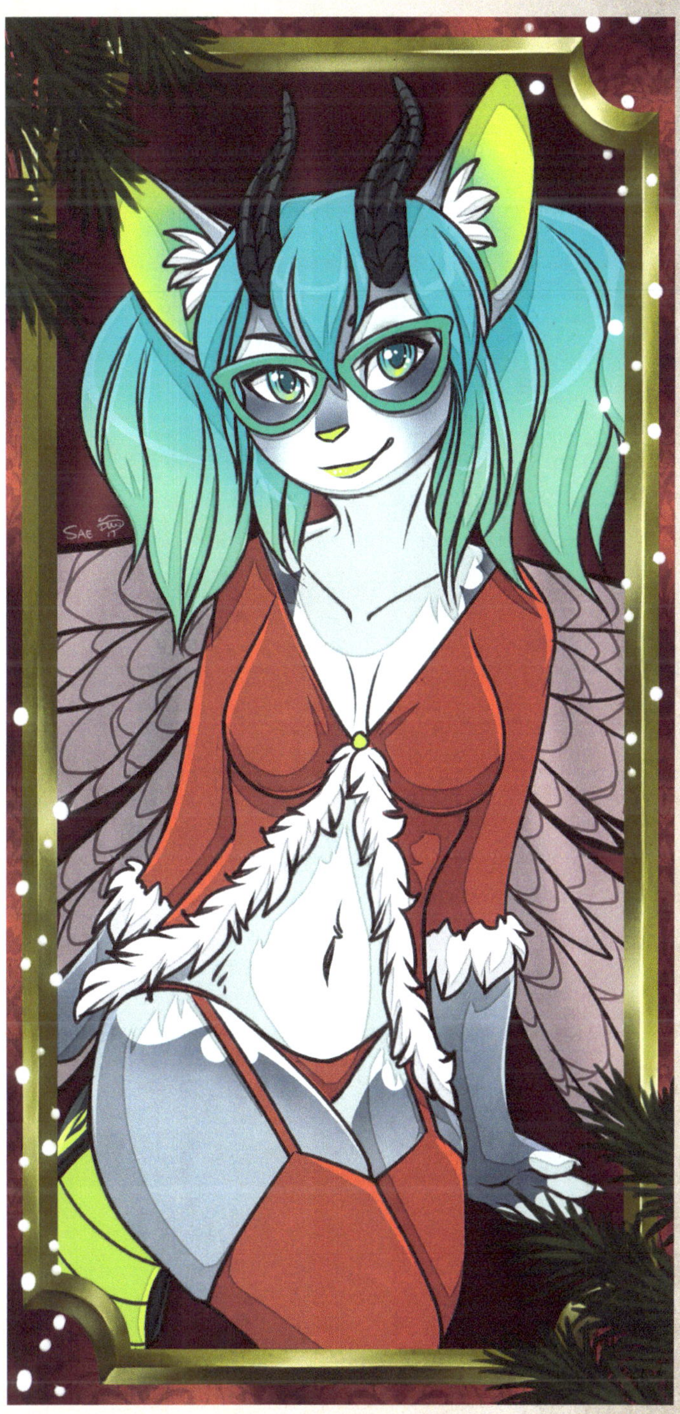

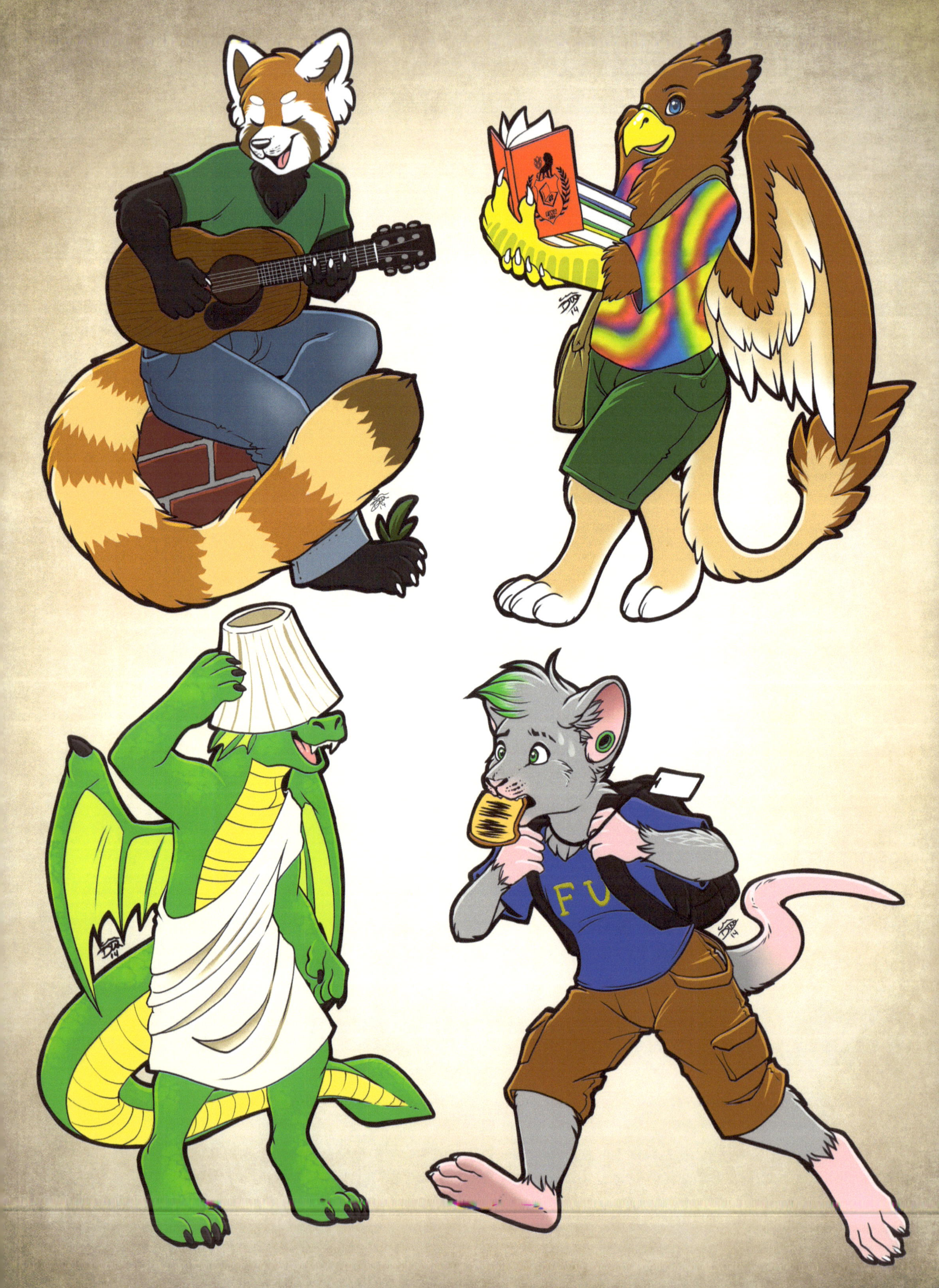
FU

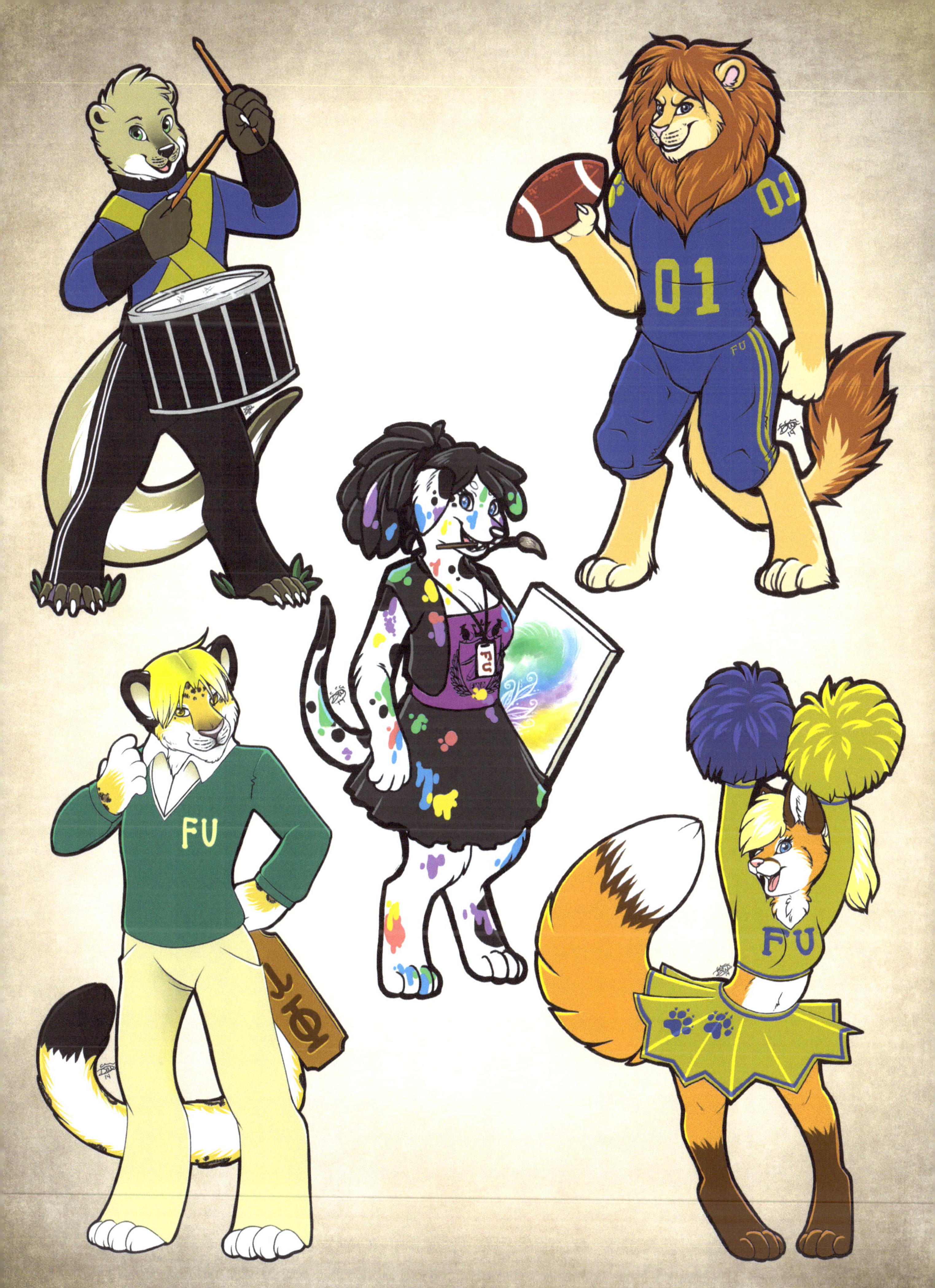
01
01
FU
FU
FU
FU

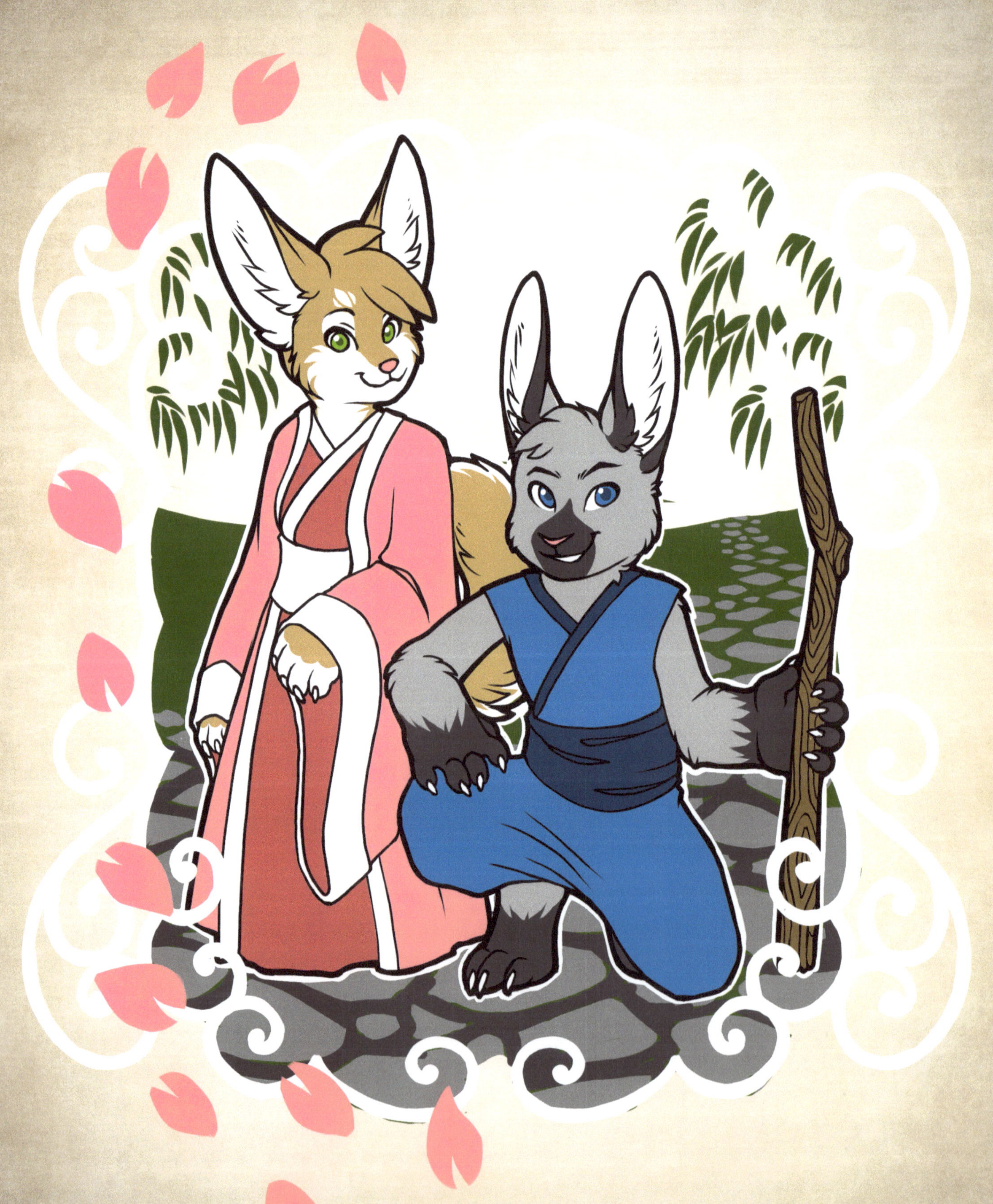

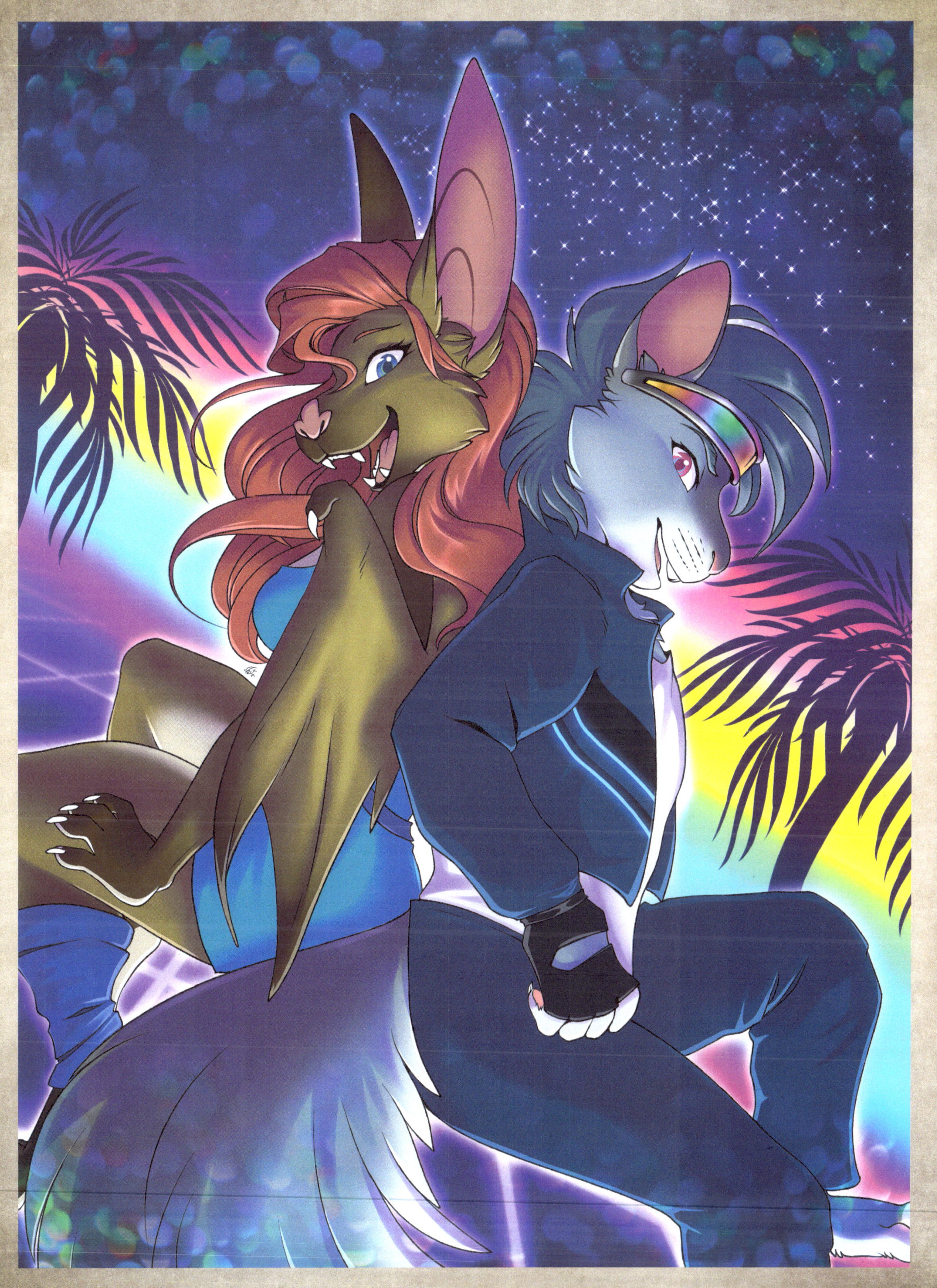

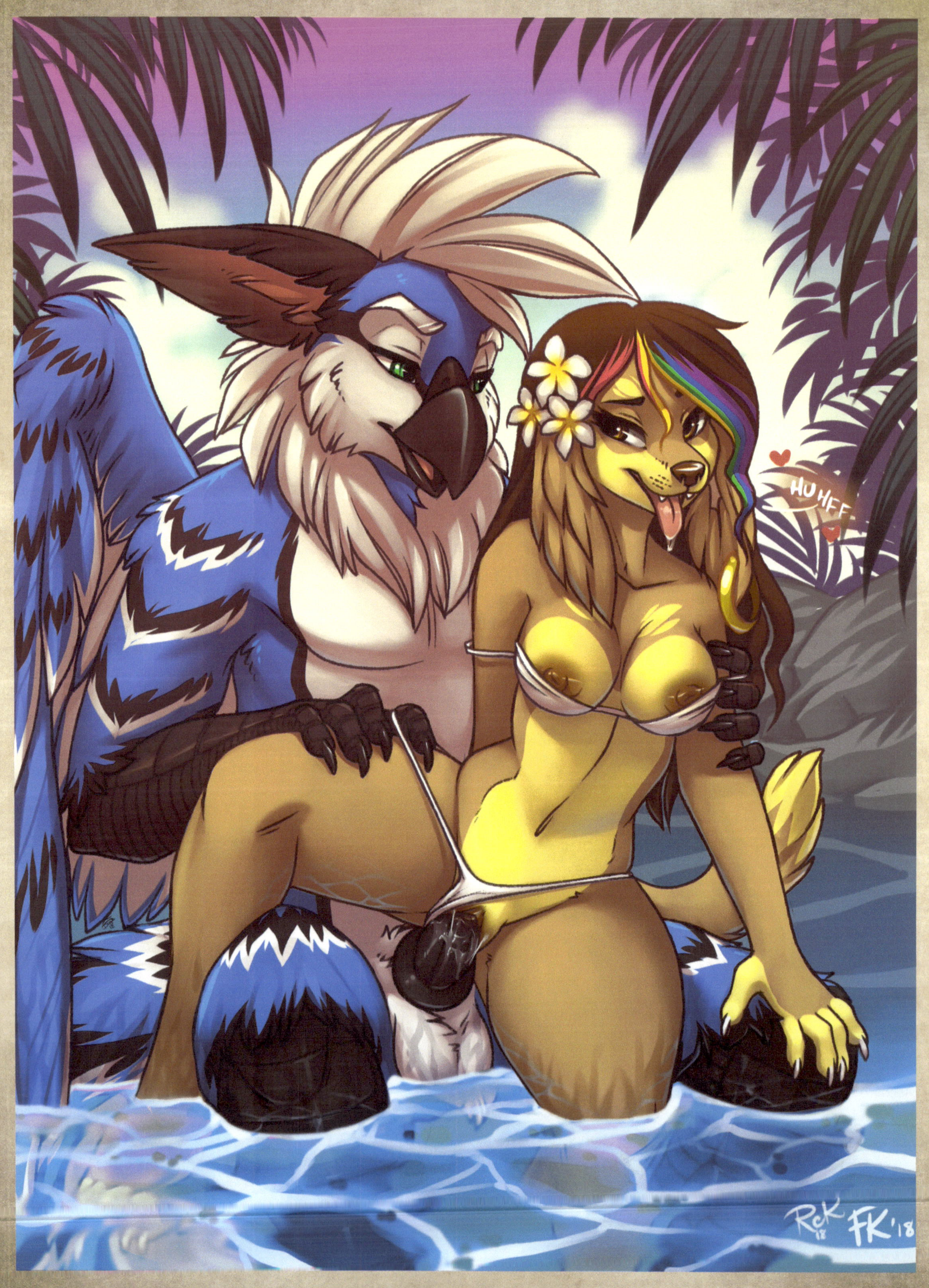
HUHFF
RcK 18
FK '18

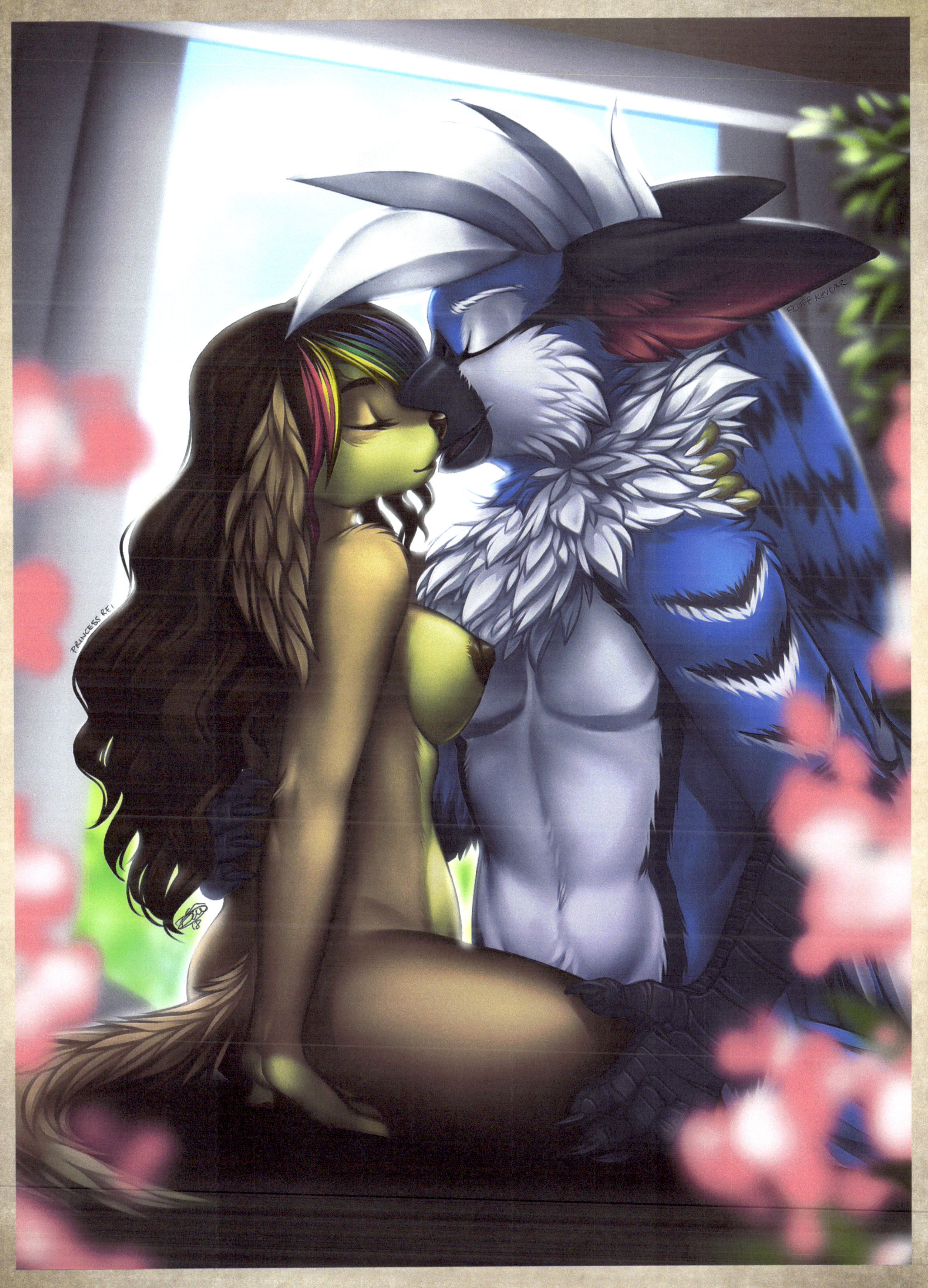
FLUFF KEVLAR
PRINCESS REI

# Thank You

*To God I give the Glory.*

Thanks to my friends, relatives, and supporters for continuing to believe in me and uplift my work. The journey is difficult, but yet, I have finally made it to book three.

Very special Thank You to Fluff Kevlar for providing both strength and tenderness throughout the healing process.

**Find me at:**
AmethystValley.com
Patreon.com/PrincessRei
Facebook.com/AmethystValley



Reimina C. Keishana

www.ingramcontent.com/pod-product-compliance
Lightning Source LLC
LaVergne TN
LVHW070136110826
845147LV00002B/261

*9781614505693*